TEN
RESPONSIBLE
MINUTES

TEN RESPONSIBLE MINUTES

A PLEASANT APPROACH TO HOMILY HEADACHES

Joseph E. Manton, C.SS.R.

AN OSV SOURCE BOOK

Our Sunday Visitor, Inc.
Huntington, Indiana 46750

ISBN: 0-87973-862-6
Library of Congress Catalog Card Number: 77-90976

Cover Design by James E. McIlrath

Published, printed and bound in the U.S.A. by
Our Sunday Visitor, Inc.
Noll Plaza
Huntington, Indiana 46750

862

CONTENTS

FOREWORD

If any man on earth should know how to write a sermon that comes to the point and, having done so, makes it, that man is Father Joe Manton. The Lord knows he has been doing it long enough, his coy pretensions to the contrary notwithstanding; moreover he has preached to tens of thousands of people of whom it is said they will not listen to sermons and have no time for them. Somehow they have managed to find the little time that Father Joe demands of them and has made them glad to come back.

A substantial part of the Back Bay section of Boston, and the hospitals and training schools found in it, have been blessed by Father Joe Manton's Wednesday afternoon and evening devotions. The writer as a student at Boston Latin School is one of thousands who crowded up Mission Hill after school each week to supplement his pre-liberal arts education under the pulpit later acclaimed for Father Joe's spiritual "responsible minutes," as his brother also journeyed up from Tufts Medical School week in and week out to get his spiritual booster shots from the same shrine.

Mission Hill is a different place now from what it was when we were at school. It used to be the land of Maurice Tobin and the Parker Hill wing of the Democratic Party. It is now a center city for all the races of the world. One thing is not changed: the "responsible minutes" which Joe Manton provided and which gave Mission Hill its name through Father Joe Manton. If we lost that — which means if we lose Father Joe — they had better level the hill!

✠ *John Cardinal Wright*

7

AUTHOR'S PREFACE

This book no more poses as a formal treatise on pulpit oratory than a neon sign over a restaurant pretends to be a rainbow.
In fact, in restaurant terms it might be summed up as a lightly
tossed salad of crisp suggestions, shredded fallacies, hard-boiled
opinions, vinegary comments, marinated memories — all served
up very informally, and across the Grand Canyon from the grim,
dry, no-nonsense pot roast of a technical treatise on preaching.

Isn't it the melancholy truth that the people who should
write the how-to books almost never do? Now if Shakespeare had
only filled a few folio pages with some points on great writing!
But, since the topflight figures generally confine themselves to
merely turning out masterpieces, it leaves the writing of the
manuals to those among us who usually have more enthusiasm
than ability.

At any rate the chapters in this book attempt to set down
some ideas on preaching picked up during a span of nearly fifty
years in the priesthood, and I pass them on for whatever they
may be worth before I hail a wheelchair and go creaking off into
the sunset. It is offered to my fellow priests with more than a little diffidence, because I have rarely faced an audience of
padres. With Redemptorists (among whom I am proud to hang
my greening biretta) the preaching of retreats to the clergy is
usually assigned to the members of the "mission band," a fraternity I secretly coveted but for which I was never tapped. On
the occasions when an invitation to conduct a priests' retreat did
flutter my way, I thought it best to give it the sweet swerve and
the velvet regret that the man who would preach to priests
should be either very holy or very learned, and with me it was

too late for the first and too soon for the second. That is why in offering these chapters I tiptoe gingerly over unfamiliar ground.

By its nature a book about preaching should be about as exciting as a worn-out sneaker or as fascinating as the middle of a bottle of glue. Anyone who has ever spent a few hours in a theological library sampling the shelves of homiletic hints comes away feeling that he has just been slogging across sand dunes in hip boots. On the other hand, there are valuable directives that should be passed on. The purpose here has been to do this not solemnly but lightly, with all the informality of a farmer's suspenders. (Who was it that said that God gave man an imagination to compensate for what he wasn't, and a sense of humor to console him for what he was?)

This, though, opens the door to the danger of the writer sounding like an "I" specialist. Nothing sickens more, floating off the printed page, than the faint whiff of the omniscient egotist. If there be any of that here, I heartily wish I could drain it off. *Personal* I should like the tone to be, but egotistic and infallible, never. I am realistically aware that I am just an average preacher, and as such, when I sometimes return to the scene of the crime and hear myself on tape, the impulse is to leave the room quickly and gulp down a couple of Dramamines, or whatever they call the pills prescribed for incipient nausea.

There may rise in the curious reader, as he reads some of the well-meant suggestions and the interspersed do's and don'ts, the mild wonder whether the writer himself practices what he preaches (about preaching). Or is he only one of Ophelia's "ungracious pastors" who generously point out to others the steep and thorny pulpit road while they themselves tread a primrose path and "reck not their own rede"? The answer to that, if I may float a loan from Lincoln, is that I do some of the things all the time, and all the things some of the time. But I could not lay an affidavit hand on *Roget's Thesaurus* and claim more. As characters like Al Capone long ago pointed out, few of us are perfect. Or even consistent.

Among us Redemptorists (there goes that commercial again!) a legend has long persisted of a veteran missionary's recipe for preaching a crashingly effective Sisters' retreat: first you examine your own conscience, then you give the nuns hell. Perhaps a little of that tactic has crept into these pages, too.

Finally (and you thought I would never get there), if you, the reader, dipping here and there in the book as the spirit moves you, should scoop up even a tiny teaspoon of benefit, I ask in return a small token prayer. If, on the other hand, you derive no good whatever, then you will know that I need prayers even more.

Joseph E. Manton, C.SS.R.

P.S. It just occurs to me to add that wherever I have borrowed, I have tried to give due credit. However, for any material that I may have unconsciously remembered and innocently rewritten, I ask absolution.

1 ● A Duty, Not a Choice

You could raise many a pious eyebrow by casually contending that the Apostles took to preaching the Gospel because they had become tired of toting trays. But if you did, it would not exactly take a Scripture scholar to nail you to the mast for deceptive oversimplification. And yet it is a curious, smiling fact that the post of deacon was established precisely because the Apostles had complained that too much of their time was taken up with waiting on tables (Acts 6:2), time they wanted to devote to prayer and preaching.

Isn't it refreshing to read, though, that they wanted to have more time for these sacred pursuits, and in that edifying order? They knew that an effective sermon needs prayer as much as a plant needs water. And is it not quite possible that this very neglect of prayer is one of the reasons why good sermons grow rarer?

To be sure, the mediocrity of the pulpit has been a perennial gripe. In nineteenth-century London, Queen Victoria, back from church one Sunday morning, noticed that her aged escort, Lord Melbourne, was dozing in his seat by the fire. This made her recall that His Lordship had nodded more than theological assent during the sermon. So the Queen said rather loudly, "My Lord, do you notice there are not many good preachers to be found these days?" My Lord came to, and countered, "But then, Madam, these days there are not many good of anything." Moses probably felt the same in his day, and Abraham in his. Everything used to be better.

Frank Sheed, that lucid writer and lively lecturer, put us pulpiteers in our proper place many years ago. He was talking from a soapbox in Hyde Park when some well-meaning chap in the crowd raised his hand for a question. "Why is it, I want to know, that so many Catholics go to church on Sunday, compared to the rest of us?" Dr. Sheed scratched his handsome head and smiled, "I can solemnly assure you that they do not go there for the sermon."

Granted, that was jolly old England, but the surveys offer thin comfort for us preachers in our own U.S. of A. Back in 1952, a *Catholic Digest* poll reported that people considered 43 percent of the sermons excellent. But in 1965, another poll revealed that the figure had slipped to 30 percent. By 1974, the milk of homiletic criticism had curdled so much that the rate was down to 22 percent, or about one sermon in five. If they continue the survey into the twenty-first century, we may end up in the minus column.

Another Catholic magazine, the *Liguorian*, ran an article in April 1975, whose author declared that a recent questionnaire sent out to army chaplains of all faiths reached the conclusion that "preaching was in a state of decline, with the sermons being generally poor, irrelevant, and unprepared."

In all fairness, I would like to bring out that at a preaching workshop for such chaplains in which I participated, the priests disagreed with this finding completely. The enthusiasm and energy they put into the sessions of that workshop were miles away from poor and unprepared sermons. They were eager; they were conscientious; they were dedicated. I have never been a chaplain. I volunteered to my superiors in World War II, but they told me to stay home and knit. But chaplain or not, I wonder why I personally have never seen one of these questionnaires that are supposedly circulated among priests. I knew only one man that got one. Put me down as a Don Quixote riding the land with the lance of a wistful pen, in quest of a questionnaire. A pity, too, because we who are never asked have all the answers.

All this is not to say that there is not, among the laity, a spreading discontent about the general quality of preaching. Perhaps with the permissiveness rampant in so many other fields, the criticism in this area grows louder and bolder. Years ago it might have been more subtle. I recall reading (this has to be twenty years back) about a club composed of young Catholic business women. They lived in the same general neighborhood, and sometimes discussed the sermons preached in their various parishes. They took turns attending different Catholic churches, and decided there were three or four fine preachers in the lot, while the others were somewhat south of mediocrity. It finally came to the point where they would sit in the back pew with poised pencil, and take down in shorthand the sermon of the able speakers. These, transcribed, they sent anonymously to the poorer preachers. The moral is that if anyone mails you any typed sermons, start thinking some long thoughts.

In our later day we do not (I hope) have such vagrant stenographers, but we surely do have some "Roamin' Catholics" who coolly drive past their own parish church and blithely point the radiator cap of the car toward a church where they feel they will hear a better homily. Perhaps it should not be that way, but unfortunately that is the way it is. They will drive five miles out of their way to find a better mouth-trap.

However, no matter how low a wattage may dimly glow in the Reverend Father's mental bulb (and it cannot be too low if he got where he did) it is probable that the average Catholic congregation is more tolerant of the talent, or lack of it, of the man in the pulpit than is a Protestant audience. Up to now, at least, priests are generally assigned to a parish, whereas ministers are invited or "called" to a more prominent pulpit precisely because they have been successful preachers somewhere else.

It is easy to snipe at the man in the pulpit. Harry Emerson Fosdick, so long the prestigious preacher of New York's Riverside Church, voiced an uneasy suspicion that the man in the pew looked up at the man in the pulpit as "a salaried propagandist for

15

a foregone conclusion." It certainly is not a flattering appraisal, and I cannot accept it as a true one.

Words are like pretzel dough, and can be bent to the will of the bender. If the crowd is on your side, it is an enthusiastic throng. If it is against you, it is a rabid mob. If an innovator is your friend, he is a courageous and forward-looking progressive. If he is your enemy, he is a dangerous and wild-eyed revolutionary.

Similarly, Dr. Fosdick's phrase can be twisted till it is straight again. "Salaried?" Are not clergymen, of all professional people, the lowest paid, even lower than school teachers? "Propagandist?" The nobler term is "crusader." And does not "foregone conclusion" really mean "ultimate truth"? See how it comes out now: the man in the pulpit emerges as the "selfless crusader for ultimate truth." That robe hangs on him more naturally.

But much more important than what the listener in the bench thinks of the role of the preacher, is what the preacher himself thinks of his office. If he reads St. Paul, he will both swell with honest pride and groan at his mountainous responsibility. That tireless little Apostle (bald of head and fiery of heart) demands that we preach the Word in season and out of season. It is not, in his eyes, a question of whether I like to preach, or even whether I have a particular talent for preaching. It is not a question of personality or disposition or inclination or built-in eloquence. It comes down solely to duty. If I am a priest, I have an obligation to proclaim the Gospel.

Whether or not I prefer Gothic or Roman vestments is a matter of taste. Whether or not I like to celebrate Mass alone or to concelebrate, is a matter of temperament. Whether the bells ring out for High Mass in my church at ten or at eleven on Sunday morning is a matter of custom or convenience. But whether I preach or not is a matter of conscience.

Preaching is the chief, if not the only, way that the message of Christ can come to men. I am His agent. I am not a salesman selling Cadillacs or cat food, but I am a soulsman, offering a product that is the Word of God, the Good News of Salvation, the Law of the Lord. But I can learn from salesmen. Our common mission is to persuade.

If, on radio or television, I see to what lengths advertisers go to put over a commercial, can I in conscience be casual or indifferent or even sloppy in presenting Christ's message? If one minute of commercial time on a Super Bowl telecast runs over a hundred thousand dollars in price, can you imagine the preparation that goes into that sixty-second appeal to buy Buick cars or Botany ties? Shouldn't the intense preparation of admen be at least a gentle spur to my conscience?

A dedicated preacher takes his stand in the pulpit not because he "has to say something," but because he has something to say. He may smilingly refer to his talk as "a few appropriate words," but he knows that this is precisely what those words should be: appropriate but not appropriated. Any man who borrows most of his material from somebody else is like a beggar who would proudly boast of his patches.

How sad it is that so many people merely take the sermon for granted! There it is; you cannot avoid it; you accept it grudgingly like the collection. It is part of the ritual, something to be endured as part of the sacrifice (with a small *s*). But as for illuminating people's minds or changing their lives — forget it.

If this is the attitude of many a person in the pew toward the talk, how did it become so? Somebody has said that there are three kinds of speakers: those you listen to, those you can't listen to, and those you can't help listening to. That last, of course, must be our goal. How obtain it? One thing is sure: it takes work. If you spend a long time preparing a short sermon, the odds are it will turn out to be a good sermon. You cannot fault preparation.

True, there was that one occasion when our Savior came into Jerusalem mounted on an ass. He can still come into people's minds and hearts riding the sorriest of human efforts. He can,

17

but He should not. Our job is to give His majestic message the decent mount it deserves.

God's Word never automatically gets the hearing it rates. It gets only the hearing that we can win for it.

If you speak for only ten minutes to six hundred people, you are taking from them one hundred hours of their time. What are you giving them in return?

But our motive for presenting a worthwhile talk should soar past mere justice to our hearers, even though many of them may have come to the church at considerable inconvenience. It should climb even above their generous trust, though they lay before us the white page of their minds for our message. It should even go beyond our own self-respect. I pity the preacher who, no matter how humble the occasion and how few the hearers, does not have his own standard of excellence. Will your words be worthy of *you*?

But the ultimate motive for preparing and delivering a decent homily goes far beyond both preacher and the people. It rises to the very throne of God. Remember that old yarn about the celebrated London actor peeking out through the theater curtain and whispering to his fellow players almost in awe, "The King is out there tonight!"

For the preacher, our King is always out there — the King of Kings!

And that is why we must always be at our best. Or at least energetically try!

2 ● Talent

Charles Wesley, that tireless trumpet of Methodism, sent the Word of God hurtling from one pulpit or another no less than forty thousand times. This, may I interject for our mutual consolation, does not imply forty thousand different manuscripts. On the contrary, the Reverend Mr. Wesley had Xerox tonsils, and loved to repeat over and over again his volcanic homilies. To him the oft-repeated sermons were the best sermons. He affectionately called them his "old soldiers."

For Wesley, the pulpit came first, the desk only second. He would deliver a talk many times, like taking a ship on several practice cruises, before he committed the sermon to the permanency of paper. But once he had written it, he never changed it. He always claimed that a new sermon on the same subject would never be so good. He had drained his brain.

If that sends your eyebrows up like awnings, listen to this. Wesley said, with no ifs, ands, or buts, that "preaching is indeed the gift of God, and cannot be attained by all the efforts of nature and art united." Doesn't that sound like the predestination of the preacher? Either you have it, or you don't. And if you don't have it, too bad!

There will be a short pause while we wave the ghost of Wesley far away, and open the windows of our mind to that good old honest try.

Out of the other corner of the courtroom comes Cardinal Manning for the defense. According to this prelate, "The sermon is a manifestation of the Incarnate Word, from the written word, by the spoken word." Translated into sidewalk English, this seems to mean that the Word of God gets to the pulpit through the desk. First you write it, then you preach it.

The trouble is that the ability to write well is also a talent all its own. Like a bell-like baritone or a Barrymore profile, it is a gift of God. Ask anyone who has taught "Creative Writing" and he will nod in wholesale agreement.

He will tell you that if the professor has, let us say, twenty students enrolled in the class, and during the very first week he hands out an assignment, perhaps three of the twenty will hand in outstanding papers. When the course ends, some months later, these same three will again turn in the best papers. These three have the gift: It is there like big blue eyes or curly blond hair. God gave it and they possess it.

How about the other seventeen? If the Prof grades their ability on the scale of one to ten, most of them will have made measurable progress. Perhaps half of them will go up as far as six or seven on the scale.

The melancholy deduction is that mere work will never blossom into spectacular talent. But just as certain is the fact that the seed of whatever talent is there, can develop in its own quiet and satisfactory way. And for the long run, especially in a calling like the priesthood, the quiet, constant bubbling spring can do more good than the occasional breathtaking geyser.

Glittering talents do not sparkle and tinkle like rows of bright medals on many sacerdotal cassocks. Occasionally there does come along a man with a handsomely carved face, shoulders broad as a billboard, a voice like thunder rolling through a canyon (only clearer), an imagination that spurts off clever phrases like a Roman candle, a warm, attractive personality, an actor's instinct for the dramatic — occasionally such a one towers above the horizon, but don't hold your breath waiting for him.

When the average priest squints sleepy-eyed into his shaving mirror in the yawning morning, he sees another image altogether. He cannot count on a strikingly impressive appearance to open his way like silver trumpets. Between what he is, and what he would like to be, lies a bridge of sighs.

So, if the jacket won't sell the book, all the more reason to see that the contents will. Each of us has, wrapped in our scriptural napkin, some kind of talent. The idea is to use what we have. By no stretch of the imagination could Rex Harrison be styled a singer, yet he carried off the leading male role in *My Fair Lady* as if he owned the stage, using his magnificent diction, his rich interpretation, his delicate sense of timing to make us forget that he was reciting, not singing. In a similar vein, Rosalind Russell made her audience forget a voice that one critic described as sounding like a lighthouse moaning to its mate. Her own self-appraisal was, "I don't sing. I gargle." Yet you forgot the want of music in the wealth of meaning that she gave her words.

Robert Benchley used to say that it took him fifteen years of slavery over a typewriter to discover that he had no talent for writing, but by that time he had become so well known as a writer that he was afraid to admit it. The truth is, of course, he did not have to admit anything. He was ironically describing how long it took the flower to unfold.

At present, the overworked word used to describe extraordinary talent is charisma. Those who have it, wear it like an invisible halo. By any name, it is the mysterious gift that leaps over the footlights to the farthest balcony, or from the pulpit to the last pew, the magic magnetism that builds an unseen bridge between a man and his audience. They say that if you have it, you don't need anything else; and if you don't have it, it doesn't matter whatever else you have. Perhaps. But how many have it? How often does a comet streak its silver glow across the sky? The Alps are more than the Jungfrau and Mont Blanc. There are foothills, too. Charisma in its true sense is most rare. Like miracles.

On those infrequent occasions when original sin rears its serpentine head and subtly suggests that after all we ourselves may have a considerable endowment of talent, God in His mercy is generally swift to deflate the blimp. (Or, for the logicians, crush the snake.) Not many years ago a newly ordained wrote to me, asking if I would preach at his First Mass. With devastating simplicity his letter concluded, "I realize this is only short notice, two weeks. But you must realize that you are the fourth priest I have approached." As the tombstone reads over the lawyer's grave: DEFENSE RESTS. That sermon I would not have missed for the world.

Only a fool spends his life yearning for the talent he does not have. The sensible man takes the talent he does have and adds toil — till the whole becomes an acceptable product. Some talent and much toil is a marriage that always produces healthy and attractive offspring. It is not like the situation when Isadora Duncan, the dancer, proposed marriage to George Bernard Shaw, suggesting that the fruit of their union would inherit her looks and his brains. Shaw demurred, fearing the child might inherit his looks and her brains.

Some talent and *much* toil have to fill the preacher's deep well, because he has to go to that well so often. The brazen calendar dares to tell you that there are seven days in each week, but any preacher knows that between Sunday and Sunday there is only a gap of about twenty minutes.

And, as if the sudden popping up of Sunday were not enough, there is the added disadvantage for most of us of having to face the same audience. It is true that they may not remember what we say, in the sense that not one out of thirty could tell us what we preached about last Sunday, but they will recognize a vivid incident or an attractive illustration, whenever we wheel it in once more.

Back in the days of Lenten courses, some curates used to form a kind of circuit-riding team. Each man wrote one sermon and then delivered it first in his own church and then in five others, during the six successive Lenten weeks. Obviously this solved the problem of having to prepare a different sermon each Wednesday night for the same congregation, by offering the same sermon to a different congregation. If you can't change the railroad, change the train. But it didn't train preachers.

Occasional sermons, in the sense of a sermon for a special occasion, have this built-in boon: they generally take you to a different place with a new congregation and a special setting. I still can remember with technicolor vividness the only parish mission I ever preached, more than thirty years ago. When you walked across the sanctuary, the very air throbbed, expectant and electric. As you looked down on the packed church (nobody missed the mission in those days), the benches leaned forward to seize your message. You came to them like a flashing meteor in the parish sky, and they looked up with eagerness and awe. (If they didn't know your name, you were "the strange priest" — not *that strange*, mind you, but only in the sense of being a stranger and not one of the old reliables.)

I could not but help contrast that rare mission experience with my regular preaching assignment, which was a weekly Wednesday novena from nine in the morning through nine at night. Through almost forty years, I stood in that same pulpit, on Wednesdays alone, nearly nine thousand times. For a score of years, it was a matter of eight novena services each Wednesday. There, when you looked down from the huge marble pulpit, you faced a congregation that just took you for granted. They were not hostile but they were not exactly panting either.

On the other hand, a familiar congregation offers this sterling benefit. They know you. They trust you. They sense that over the long stretch you are trying to do your best and they appreciate it. You have established credibility and respect. They accept you. They probably like you. You may not have been a brilliant patent-leather pump (as we viewed the symbol of elegance in an older day), but you were a comfortable old shoe. And they wouldn't want to be without you. Not *me*. *You*, in your regular pulpit.

To get back, though, to the matter of talent and toil. Father Elliot, a veteran Paulist parish missionary of the early twentieth century, used to wither young confreres who moaned that they had no preaching talent. His argument ran something like this: "You say you cannot preach. But you can talk politics with enthusiasm and power. You can run down a neighboring pastor as if you were a prosecuting district attorney. And when it suits you, you can blast the bishop till you all but turn his miter inside out. You can be articulate and persuasive and dynamic in talking about your favorite football or baseball team. But you cannot preach. Nonsense! You can preach. You just don't!"

Admittedly, there may be here a bit of what the philosophers used to call *latius hos*, because for a good sermon you need more than conviction and enthusiasm. A young man may love his bride with every fiber of his being, but that does not equip him to deliver a brilliant half-hour oration on her beauty or his love.

It comes down to this: public speaking requires private preparation. Your conviction is one thing; your ability to express it, is a car from another garage. Ask any successful author, and he will wryly point to his leaning tower of rejection slips. The shining statue of eventual achievement stands on the dull pedestal of much previous work.

But your complacent preacher tends to be satisfied with the mediocre. Because nobody boos or throws bottles, he is in danger of quietly presuming that he "is not so bad," meaning, on his scale, rather good. But while his self-confidence soars like an Alpine peak, his accomplishment stays an anthill. He needs to read and write and then write some more; but instead, he just stands up and talks. His coldest critic should make him a birthday gift of a tape recorder.

When Cicero was asked what is the straightest path to oratory, he answered simply, *"Scribere quam plurimum!"* ("Write as much as possible!") Though St. Augustine had written a shelf of books, to his last days he still felt the need of writing each sermon.

24

Sinclair Lewis once began a lecture on writing to an earnest group of would-be authors: "So you want to become good writers? Then why aren't you home writing?"

By swimming we learn to swim — not by buying a pair of flippers and a book. The book may provide some helpful pointers, but there is no substitute for practice. In sermon writing we call it preparation, which is just a longer word for work.

As to the talent part, our patron saint should be the boy with the basket of loaves and fishes on that New Testament hillside. Was anything more ridiculous than coming to Christ with so little for so many — five loaves for five thousand people? But our Lord did not spurn the offering. He accepted it. He made use of it. And so will He do with our talent, small as it may seem. He is God, and with our few loaves He can work wonders. But with loafers not even He can do much.

3 ● How Else Will They Know?

In some religious sects, the preaching pennant ripples so high on the mast of clerical duties that the clergyman is not called the pastor or the parson or the priest or the minister, but simply and solely the preacher. It was possibly to one of these that the stolid traffic cop was handing a routine ticket. "But, Officer, I am only a poor preacher." "I know," answered the policeman. "I've heard you."

Poor or not, preaching has generally been regarded in most religions as of paramount importance. In the Catholic Church, Vatican II has given the pulpit its own special salute of recognition. Before that, if anyone had asked me which was the principal duty of a Catholic priest, I should have automatically rattled off, "To offer the Sacrifice of the Mass and to dispense the sacraments." But now I know. To my admitted amazement, the opening paragraph of Vatican II's document on "The Ministry of Priests" declares that priests "have as their *primary duty* the proclamation of the Gospel."

This is not to whittle away one sliver from the sublimity of the Mass. In another section of the Council text, the offering of the Eucharist is set down as "the priest's chief duty." It needs perhaps a pharmacist's delicate scales to calibrate the difference between "primary duty" and "chief duty"; but how often has preaching been placed in such high company? Apparently the Church wants us to realize that unless the Gospel has been proclaimed, then neither Mass nor sacraments will have any meaning.

Without preaching, how can the People of God know their obligations toward Him and their responsibilities toward one another? Is anyone naïve enough to suggest that the answer lies in spiritual books? Those of us who have written a few are grimly aware how small a group we reach. Wasn't it Don Marquis who sourly observed that publishing a slim volume of poetry and expecting a response was like dropping a rose leaf into the Grand Canyon and waiting for the echo? You can say the same about the average spiritual book that treats Christian virtue, or the life of a saint, or a look into the liturgy. Anti-celibacy tracts (in which the "new breed" intimate they would like to do a little breeding) may sell; but with the ordinary spiritual book the ripples rarely reach out beyond a small circle of unusually pious people.

Or, do you feel that, as the proper Bostonian ladies "had their hats" (from God knows when), so the run-of-the-mill Catholic has his religion, having learned it in his catechism, and so needs no more "input"? Didn't he go to a parochial school or a Sunday School or even the Confraternity of Christian Doctrine?

Perhaps. Or, if you prefer, he surely did. But just as surely has he not gradually forgotten most of what he learned? Religious information is the same as any other kind of information. It fades away. Time lays its layer of dust on what once was shining knowledge. For that matter, once we knew the products of Paraguay and the exports of Ecuador and the curious intricacies of cube root. (At least in my remote day, we were drilled in all these in that huge red-brick Brooklyn parochial school.) But how many of us would enthuse about an extensive quiz on these subjects now? So many things melt with the snows of yesteryear!

From Sunday to Sunday, an able priest strives to offer a refresher course in religion. He goes back to the basics, but not with annoying obviosity. He tries to preach as if his audience had never heard. "How shall they believe in Him of whom they have never heard? Or how shall they hear without a preacher?"

Our Savior was the preacher par excellence. In the wilderness He preached so glowingly that they forgot their need for food so that He had to multiply bread to feed the multitude. On the lakeside He preached so persuasively, and they pressed so close about Him, that He had to make His pulpit the prow of Peter's ship.

In view of His example, who can undercut the importance of preaching? Was it not preaching that founded the Faith in the days of the Apostles, and that maintains the Faith in contemporary parishes, and that carries the Faith through the sermons of missionaries to non-Christian lands?

The Fathers of the Church used to say that community prayer was the people speaking to God, but that preaching was God speaking to His people. From that should we not draw the awesome conclusion that when we preach we are the human cable bringing the commands of God down to His creatures? Each of us, standing in a pulpit, is a transmitting tower for the message of the Almighty. We become, each one of us, a kind of minor prophet.

Phillips Brooks, whose statue stands in stately bronze before Boston's picturesque Trinity Church, added a fascinating detail to that image. He felt that a fine sermon was the truth of God shining through the prism of the preacher's individual personality. In other words, here is the message of God, coming from on high like the sun; there are you, the preacher, catching the Light and diffusing it in your own vivid colors among the people.

Henry Ward Beecher, who, far from being a Boston Brahmin, hailed from Brooklyn (which a few of us hold a certainly higher honor), believed that the goal of every sermon should be either the making or the mending of men. What preacher worthy of his salt-water gargle can approach the pulpit with a stifled yawn if he realizes that in God's plan, he is to be the channel between heaven and humanity?

Wendell Phillips set down the purpose of a sermon as he saw

it: "The theater amuses, the press instructs, the pulpit improves." From the valley, to the plateau, to the peak!

If a priest has no higher privilege than to offer the Sacrifice of the Mass, he has no higher responsibility than to preach the Word.

4 ● Different Men, Different Methods

A preacher is:

1. *An idea.* (The topic that begets the thought.)
2. *A word.* (The style that packages the thought.)
3. *A voice.* (The instrument that projects the thought.)
4. *A man.* (The personality that colors the thought.)

At first glance, you might think that all of the above is a kind of oratorical silk hat that could set just as formally on the head of a university lecturer. There is, however, a deep chasm of difference between lecturer and preacher. It is not quite the difference between a dry textbook and a rousing hymnbook, but it points in that direction. While the two trails may sometimes cross, the *prime* purpose of the lecturer is to inform, while that of the preacher is to inspire. The lecturer tells you what you did not know; the preacher tells you what you ought to do. It was summed up best by that preacher who said, "When I stand in the pulpit, I want to make the indifferent people different."

Different, presumably, from the casual Christians or the practical pagans that live on every street. The concerned preacher holds high the banner of faith and calls for believing souls to rally round it. Though he knows that this sad world is, by and large, enemy territory, he speaks out fearlessly because he knows that the power of God stands behind him.

It is something like that incident in ancient Libya where, far out on the desert, there was quartered a tiny Roman garrison. One day the cavalry of a barbarian army came pounding toward it. The Roman commander stood in front of his little squad of men, traced a line with his sword across the sandy soil, and said, "Here is Caesar's. Pass this line and you attack the empire of Rome." The barbarian chieftain, whose force could have annihilated the small outpost, reined in his horse and swung his troops off in another direction.

Behind the resolute preacher of God's Word rises up the might of the Almighty. As the representative of the Lord, and the attorney who pleads the case for Christ, the preacher knows that justice and right are on his side, and he need never cut compromising corners. He must speak out as clearly and confidently as a trumpet.

If God is behind him, and the congregation literally in front of him, the preacher automatically becomes the middleman between God and the people. And, if the power of God is to give muscle to his words, the lives of the people will provide topics for his talks. For this reason he must mingle among them, be part of them, never hold himself aloof from them. They will not eagerly hear a preacher who lives in an ivory tower and delivers his sermons from a library ladder. Exit the ineffectual intellectual!

Only in a stained-glass window do you see a gorgeously robed Christ preaching to three or four radiant figures in picturesquely attentive poses. Read the Gospels themselves, and you find Christ in the midst of the crowd, the peasant crowd, sweaty and breathy and weirdly fragrant in the days when deodorants were still far beneath the horizon.

Clerical contact, to be sure, need not be that intimate or physical, but into the homes of his people the good priest goes and learns about their lives. He gets to know them, but not like the postman, who gets no farther than the mailbox. The good pastor goes into the very heart of the home where he sees at firsthand their struggles and their problems, their sicknesses and their sorrows, their disappointments and their discouragements, their secret worries and their unspoken dreams, their unexpected little joys, their high hopes and their deep fears, their whole little world that revolves behind the window curtains.

A priest who knows his people like this will be listened to. His every word will be illumined by the bright lantern of personal experience and will be warmed by the glowing fire of an understanding heart.

New York's Harry Emerson Fosdick whose voice from the Riverside Church's pulpit was for years as familiar and famous as the carillon from its tower, felt that his main job as a preacher was not to illuminate a subject but to move an audience. Wherever possible, he liked to give the impression that his sermon was an animated conversation between pews and pulpit — with him, to be sure, playing both roles. For illustrations and stories, he borrowed from the portrait gallery of history. Facts about the famous, he maintained, furnished appealing and persuasive arguments for the man in the street. It flattered Mr. Ordinary and induced him to try to do likewise himself.

Another well-known preacher of our day was Dr. James Pike, the late Episcopal bishop of San Francisco. (In any art, from painting to piano, you learn from the masters. You may not admire them as men, but you marvel at their technique. And if you cannot study under them, you can at least learn from them.) Anyway, Bishop Pike is unusual because he complained that in the seminary he had been coached into acquiring an "elegant" style. His reaction against this was so great that in his mature years he repudiated writing as a tool for the preparation of a sermon. This soars up, like a kind of Eiffel Tower exception, among the attitudes of most great preachers.

Note, however, this. Bishop Pike did not reject *preparation*, but his preparation was mostly in the head, or in the words he fed into the tape recorder, and then listened to. He might write the talk *after* he had delivered it, often polishing it for publication, but you get the impression from his lectures on preaching that writing was not a heavy gun in his oratorical battery. He laid more emphasis on the delivery.

Bishop Pike had the strange conviction (but with him it apparently worked) that if you thought deeply and intensely about your Sunday morning sermon before you went to sleep on Saturday night, "the dough put in the oven before going to bed would turn out to be pretty good biscuits in the morning." This seems first cousin to the theory you sometimes hear about learning a foreign language by putting a tape recorder under your pillow and absorbing the material while you sleep. Personally, I would hate to bank on it.

But don't deceive yourself that Bishop Pike dozed himself into an eloquence that consistently filled his cathedral. In preparing for a sermon, he first read and read and read, and scribbled all manner of notes, and spoke endlessly into his recorder. To make himself prepare, he always had the theme of next Sunday's sermon announced in this Sunday's bulletin. That way he could not grow lazy and reach back into the bin and offer the rerun of an oldie. The announced title also piqued the curiosity of the people.

Bishop Pike always claimed that somehow people with the very problem he was going to discuss on the following Sunday, would saunter into his rectory during the preceding week, and give him the ammunition he needed. Could it not be that the topic announced in the bulletin had been a subtle invitation?

Archbishop Fulton Sheen would discourage, if not dismay, the average priest in the area of sermon preparation. He has said that for seven Lenten sermons (each presumably about a half hour's length), he spent a total of four hundred hours. This works out to eight hours a day for a full week. That total, to be sure, included the many hours spent meditating upon his theme. In fact, he smilingly subjoined that after the planning and the thinking of the topic, there remained only one trifling detail: the writing. Most of us will just watch such an eagle spiral into the sky and enviously wave him to the heights.

The archbishop, though, is in fine company with a couple of cardinals. Cardinal Manning in his *Eternal Priesthood* and

Cardinal Gibbons in his *Ambassador of Christ* both emphasize the importance of the remote as against the immediate preparation. They maintain that if a man had been a good student in the seminary, and was now a studious and prayerful priest, then from the twin fountains of his knowledge and his piety would flow extemporaneous sermons that would be simple, direct and moving.

Far be it from a sparrow to dare to disagree with these high-flying hawks, but I must confess that though my theological training was reasonably adequate, and my present goodwill hopefully genuine, that word "extemporaneous," even in its broadest connotation, gives me oratorical chills. I can only confess that, after nearly five decades of preaching, if I were called upon for a sermon on short notice, I would either gratefully unwrap the mummy of some ancient effort, or would offer my high regards and deep regrets. Undoubtedly there are those that can come up with an abrupt and on-the-spot masterpiece, but I know I shall never take my place in that bright and blessed band.

Or, as the fellow said, "What we need today is more men like St. Teresa!"

Father James Gillis could make research look like spontaneity. He was (the graybeards among us will remember) that famous Paulist who shared the coast-to-coast radio program *Catholic Hour* with Fulton Sheen back in the thirties. He was also the crusading editor of *The Catholic World*. In those days, the latter was put down, at least in my Philistine circle, as being written by and for school teachers. By that, we meant it was prissy and proper, dignified, didactic and alas, dull. Father Gillis' ambition was to lift it to the literary level of a Catholic *Harper's* or *Atlantic Monthly*.

Everybody I knew, read it for the editorials. Father Gillis scorned the editorial "we." He came to battle bearing before him the straight steel lance of the perpendicular and responsible pronoun "I." In those days, most Catholic magazine writing was "pretty," a sort of embroidered piety, as dainty as a Japanese painting on silk. Father Gillis came along with hammer and chisel and carved his opinions on stern, strong granite. In his hand a pen lengthened out into a bayonet, and a typewriter began to rattle like a machine gun. Often he stood alone in his opinion as on some isolated hill, holding out against the popular view of the moment. Reactions against him were at times so bitter that he offered to resign as editor so as not to embarrass his fellow Paulists.

To their credit, they declined. But, after ten years as a speaker on the *Catholic Hour* radio program, he was abruptly dropped. They never told him why, and he told me it hurt him to the heart. I have sometimes thought that when he, the best known of the Paulists, and St. Paul himself met in heaven, they probably compared wounds. They were both fighters. With both, it was go or stop; they knew no amber for caution.

Father Gillis' theory of preaching was simple. He never worried about such questions as, "What will the clergy think?" Or, "What will the highbrow critics write?" But only, "Will it hit home in the pews?" He could have been profound and erudite and polished and subtle, so that arty admirers would have swung the perfumed censer of adoring flattery. But the people needed what was practical, and he was determined to serve the people.

He prepared for his sermon by reading; but that reading meant anything except sermon books. These left him faintly nauseous. A treatise from a theology textbook, a chapter from history, a few articles from the encyclopedia — such were the kind of logs he tossed on the fire that was always blazing in his brain. As he read, he wrote furiously rapid notes, setting down facts from the books, and jotting down ideas that leaped into his lively and fertile mind.

Usually he found that he had gathered too much material, so the first order of business was to discard the second-rate surplus. Then came the job of arranging the rest in a persuasive and climactic order. The only thing he really wrote, in the sense of polished sentences, were the connectives between the various arguments, like the couplings on a long freight.

At this point, he would read and reread his copy; and then read and reread again; and perhaps again and again, all the while pacing and thinking and thinking and pacing. Finally, he would thrust the crumpled sheets into a desk drawer and head for the church. Personally, it would not be enough for me. I would have spent my time memorizing the manuscript as well as I could. But to Father Gillis memorizing meant mental paralysis.

It seems that way back in seminary days, when he had stood up to speak in public for the first time, the speech he had memorized (or thought he had) went completely out of his head. He stammered, blushed and left the platform utterly humiliated. At his next attempt the following month, speaking with a faraway look in his eyes as if he were reading from a distant page, he reached the third paragraph, and then suddenly everything went blank.

A month later, when his turn came again, feeling there was nothing to lose, he tried a completely different tactic.

He wrote the speech, and read it over and over till he felt it had sunk deep into his brain. Now he could tell himself, "I am master of my topic. I do not need memory." To his surprise and delight, he found that he could confidently stand on this preparation as on a solid platform and speak out fluently and fearlessly. As a matter of fact, his classmates broke out into enthusiastic applause.

Now the young Gillis knew. From that day he never memorized, and never felt the least stage fright. He went on to become one of the nation's most sought-after speakers. And the moral? Perhaps the scriptural, "Let him who can take it, take it!" For myself, once again I admire from afar, and eat my heart out with envy (Tums are little help) and go on to plod the humbler, prosaic path of almost slavish memory. God made us all different.

Here, not as a model, but merely as a diffident suggestion, I offer the method that suits me. You try it at your own risk, with no warranty attached, no money-back guarantee.

I begin by trying to think myself empty about the selected topic. When I was younger, it was easier, and the ideas used to build up like water rising behind a dam about to burst. As they come, you scribble them down. In later years, the thoughts just trickle in, and the tendency is to panic and wonder if you will ever come up with anything at all.

The next step is go to "the files" (more about that later) and judiciously copy the best items you have culled. After that, I may look up several books that deal with the theme and copy down more facts or quotations or examples or illustrations that I may encounter.

By this time from my own mind, plus previous clippings already stored up and from various authorities or source books, I have a couple of typewritten pages of mostly one-liners, suggestive rather than exhaustive. Looking over the material, I shall probably find that it divides itself by content into different divisions or headings.

Suppose for example the topic being worked up is "The Abuse of Liquor," or, for brevity, let's just call it, "Drink." I find I have something about the causes of drink, something about the effects, something about the victims, something about the remedies. On the margin, I write a big A alongside any material relating to the causes; B for effects, C for victims and D for remedies.

Then I collect on another piece of paper all the A's. I try to figure out their best logical order, and so grade them, as $A1, A2, A3$.

I do the same with the B's, C's and D's. Then I transpose them all in the right order to a final page. By this time, there is a complete skeleton of a talk that needs only to be fleshed out or upholstered with smooth sentences and vivid details.

Many preachers, I feel sure, would shake their heads sadly

over this method, pointing out that I am driving the car in reverse. They mean that I first gather the material, and only then from it deduce and devise a sketch. They themselves would opt for the exact opposite procedure. They would say it is more logical (and perhaps it is) to design the sketch first and then go out and get the steel beams and the cement blocks for the building.

As we used to say in my native Brooklyn, "Yuh pays yer money an' yuh takes yer cherce!"

The beauty is that both ways work — if the worker is willing. Willing to work. Having decided on a topic, you can begin by either going after pertinent material or by sketching out a plan. It really should not divide us into Montagues and Capulets, or Guelphs and Ghibellines, or even Thomists and Molinists. Do we not enjoy the glorious freedom of the sons of God?

Which is another way of saying that oratory is, after all, not an exact science, and there are few things in these chapters that I would defend passionately. Perhaps only three: the need of preparation before a talk, unity in it and a clear diction when presenting it. All the rest is just fringes and tassels. But, ah, that "rest" can be what makes it oratory: the difference between the merely acceptable and the utterly enthralling.

5 ● Blaming the Seminary

In the seminary that I attended we were taught everything about the Faith except how to present it. We were carefully prepared for almost anything except effective preaching. With that reservation, it was a complete and (in retrospect) an admirable and almost awesome general training.

The building itself was a grim, gray fortress, high above the blue Hudson, about twenty miles above West Point. In fact, passengers on the "Day Liner" would look up at the huge granite building and say, "There's West Point!" But someone else would correct them and say, "No, that's Sing Sing." Perhaps there was a little truth in each error.

Sociologists called that era the "Flaming Twenties," but in our seminary it could have been right after the Council of Trent. In those days nobody ever dreamed of such things as "a temporary vocation" or "a qualified commitment," or "a leave of absence." We signed up forever.

To the young men emerging from the seminary in this post-Vatican II era, we might have looked smilingly naïve. To them we should have come out of those hallowed halls not wearing a Roman collar and carrying a gilt-edged breviary, but wearing a Buster Brown collar and carrying a Mother Goose book.

The fact is that our seminary training was the equivalent, in the spiritual order, of the Marine Corps boot camp. It was rugged, rigorous discipline, geared to prepare us against the day when our enemy would be the world, the flesh and the devil. Not necessarily in that order.

For those six years we slept under the same roof every single night, except for those three glorious nights that in anticipation at least, stood out like mountain peaks above a monotonous plain. This was the trio of nights in our last year, when each of us returned to his home parish to celebrate his First Mass. Even those three nights we spent in a Redemptorist rectory, if there was one. During our six years of training we never left the seminary, even for a summer vacation. During the six weeks in July and August when we were free from class, we were still tethered to the seminary grounds, except for picnics on the river or walks into the hills, but always home for night prayers.

During the whole six years we never ate in a restaurant, had a cigarette, or a bottle of beer, or ever saw a newspaper, or a magazine (except religious ones). We never heard a radio. From the time I was nineteen till I was twenty-five I never had a telephone in my hands. (AT&T, how did you ever survive? My father was a lineman, too.)

Meanwhile our college contemporaries were out there wearing raccoon coats, dancing the Charleston, driving third-hand Stutz Bearcats, sneaking a little nip from a silver flask on the hip (it was Prohibition, of course) and sometimes even being arrested by Elliot Ness.

As for us, we groped out of bed to the icy whir of an electric gong at five o'clock every morning. At ten in the evening we collapsed into bed when the same bell sounded "Lights out!" In between, besides the uncompromising academic routine, we did not miss a note on the ascetical scale. Our routine day included two meditations of a half hour each, Holy Mass, a visit to the Blessed Sacrament, the way of the cross, rosary, a half hour of spiritual reading, and, of course, morning and night prayers. We had a half-day's silent retreat every week, a full day every month, and ten days every year. They tried to make us men of prayer.

We had the usual athletics, all intramural, to be sure; and football was only of the touch-tackle variety. I smile as I write that, remembering that the septuagenarian priest living in the room next to mine at this writing, had to have his jaw wired after one of those "touch" games.

Curiously, or maybe not curiously at all, they were for us gloriously happy years. Today, for a grumpy old fogey who fears that the next step of "progress" may be to make seminaries co-ed, there is this pipeful of consolation: our ordination picture shows thirty-seven young faces. Now we are old, and the faces creased, and only two years away from a golden jubilee of priesthood, but you do not have to mark an X across any face. Every one of them is serving as a priest today or was buried in his vestments.

I must apologize for this digression. Nostalgia makes a poor navigator and tends to take you far off course. I had been saying that our course in homiletics was somewhat south of pathetic. If the curriculum had been a magnificent mansion, homiletics would have been the broom closet. We received no instruction whatever in how to compose a sermon. In fact until the vacation of our sixth and final year we were sternly forbidden even to try to write a sermon. To have done so would not have sent one off to a spiritual Siberia, as would have the smoking of a cigarette (I never saw one smoked in all my time) but it still was strictly a no-no. Sermon writing was for the "second novitiate," six months of spiritual renewal and sermon composition after the seminary. But quite a few, like myself, did not make that second novitiate till several years after ordination.

We did have an "elocution class" for one hour a week. Because of the large classes (we "doubled up" for elocution) you got to speak in public just once a year for ten minutes. That means that in six whole years you had to write only enough material for one total hour. This, mind you, for men who were to spend their lives preaching, as surgeons spend their lives operating, or musicians playing.

Do you realize what long neglect can do to a man's facility with words? You kept your imagination and your fluency in the camphorous depths of your trunk during the whole seminary course. At least it should have meant that. But, praise the Lord, we had a peerless teacher in elocution named Father John Waldron, who refreshed for us the rudiments of style and introduced us to the art of delivery. But even more than that, he encouraged us to form groups of three or four to meet once a week in some spare classroom. There we would stand up every Thursday (our recreation day was Thursday, not Saturday) and deliver what we had written. In this way we exercised our voices by speaking, and we exercised our patience by listening.

At least we became accustomed to writing regularly and standing up bravely and speaking out boldly. It also provided (one's peers can be very frank) a fine infiltration course before we got on the actual battlefield of the pulpit. We came to take criticism for granted. It went with the speech, like washing the dishes after a meal.

These weekly ten-minute talks were particularly beneficial to those of us who were not in demand for the several plays staged in the seminary each year. My own dramatic career was confined to two plays, one in the minor seminary and the other in the major, and in both instances the cast was composed entirely of seminarians who had never been in a play before. It was a command performance in the sense that the priest-prefects had done the commanding and tapped the wallflowers to literally get them into the act.

With the years, thank God, all this has changed. The present prospectus in our seminary offers a dozen courses in voice development, sermon composition, pulpit management. Every week the seminarians leave what were our cloistered walls to conduct catechism classes or CCD programs. They turn out religious tapes for the local radio stations. They have video equipment so a man can not only hear himself but see himself. And why not? St. Augustine asks somewhere, "Why should the devil have all the best tunes?" Or tools? Why should not the priests of tomorrow be trained in the skills of writing and speaking and radio and television technique? Are they not salesmen for Christ our Lord?

Pentecost and its miraculous oratory happened only once. Our age is the "Sundays *after* Pentecost" (in the old arrangement) when the Holy Spirit wants us to share the burden. And the burden is hard work. Otherwise the pulpit would become not a mini-Pentecost but the old Tower of Babel — or babble.

The seminarians of today do not have our alibi of yesterday. Thank God for that! So, of them much more can be expected.

6 ● Castle of the Coward?

In our Redemptorist minor seminary we had a professor who was convinced that the old Romans were fond of "qu" sounds. If you handed in a Latin theme beginning, *"Quae quidem, Quirites,"* or the like, you were in. Perhaps he siphoned his notion out of Quintilian, the Roman rhetorician, who is more widely known for his "three purposes," the goals that should motivate a speech. According to Q., these were, *placere, docere, movere*, that is, "to please, to teach, to move."

His "to please," however, did not mean to entertain. It meant to establish goodwill, right from the start. That sage advice, like twenty-four-carat gold, has not lost its value with the years. If you want the audience to heed you, you had first better make them like you. There are exceptions, but they are just that. Marc Antony winning over a hostile crowd at the bier of Caesar is a fair example of building up acceptance.

On a homelier plane, the younger Father John Frawley, C.SS.R., whom I watched in the pulpit the way a young resident watches the chief surgeon at the operating table, was both an advocate and example of that *placere* approach, or gaining goodwill. I call him "the younger" to distinguish him from his octogenarian uncle of the same name. They are both gone, these several years, to that serene land where there are no sermons to thunder and no laryngitis to fear.

I shall never forget the time when the younger Father Frawley and I were walking through the parish on the day he had been named pastor. His uncle, you should know, had been pastor there many years before. The latter had been a huge monument of a man with a flowing mane of white hair and a voice like a cathedral organ. Anyway, we stopped to say hello to a nice old lady and I introduced her to our new pastor. "Tell me," she said to him, all simplicity and sweetness, "are you anything to the *real* Father Frawley?" The present Father Frawley blinked and gulped and then said, "He was my grandfather."

At any rate, from somewhere he had inherited a grasp of crowd psychology before the word was minted or at least was in general circulation. "If they like you," he used to say, "you can tell them almost anything, and they will accept it, because they sense that you love them and want what is best for them. Put them in a genial, receptive mood, tickle them under the chin, and then you can swing from the ankles."

It is true. Two preachers can deliver essentially the same message. One will be kindly received and the other resentfully rejected. Long ago somebody called the pulpit "the castle of the coward." Does anyone doubt that at times it has been occupied by some ranting bully who used his position to blast mercilessly, knowing that there was no chance for rebuttal, and that he stood safe behind the great shield of a traditional, reverent silence? If you except the occasional whiskey-fragrant drunk (soon whisked out by a couple of burly ushers) how often have you heard any pulpit statement contested?

Not, of course, that it should be. It is a pulpit, not a panel or a town meeting. But shame on the man who takes advantage of his solo enthronement to say things in cruel sarcasm or raging anger that never should have been said at all!

We are made up so curiously that when we mock or sneer or belittle or wax sarcastic, the words and the tones seem to come more readily. Any columnist knows it is much easier to write a piece that condemns. But the pulpit's purpose is not to condemn but to convert.

It is not hard to understand the half-playful, half-serious attitude of the dentist who filled his pastor's mouth with wad and mirror and saliva ejector and sundry instruments, all the while asking him a patter of trivial questions, which the pastor tried helplessly to answer. "Just wanted you to understand, Padre," the dentist said, "how it is with us on Sunday morning when you talk and we can't answer back."

But, if a sermon is by necessity a monologue and not a dialogue, he is a wise preacher who encourages comment from the pews at the proper time and in the proper place. If the comment is honest, the right time might be when the preacher is sitting down. Never ask an honest man for his opinion unless you are prepared for a shock. That very popular preacher, Father Pardow, who belonged to the Jesuits (quite another network), would gratefully listen to any suggestion, whether it came from an altar boy or an abbot.

"But," a very successful trial lawyer advised me once, "never ask a woman what she thought of your sermon. If it was bad, you may only get a honeyed evasion. They are constitutionally unable to tell the truth." I do not hold with him in that conviction, of course, but to be safe I have followed his counsel. Pick out a few somber-looking men in different parts of the church. They may be reluctant, but they will probably give you the truth. It may result in so simple but so important a detail as turning up the volume on the mike for the remaining Masses.

Or it may be that you have to be more vivid in your style and more varied in your delivery. But at least you will know. Feedback from the pews, humbly sought, thoughtfully evaluated, industriously acted upon, has shaken many a man from the serene but silly delusion that he was the poor man's Fulton Sheen.

We were talking about the "castle of the coward." But there is another side to the medal. If the pulpit is not a sentry box from which to fire sniping shots of personal spleen, neither is it the hiding place for Father Milquetoast. We should not be arrogant or insolent, but on the other hand we dare not be cowardly or timid. The preacher's attitude should be, "Like all human beings I am only a sinful man, but when I stand in the pulpit, I stand and speak as an ambassador of the Almighty. I speak with courage because I am a courier of Christ, bringing not my feathery personal opinion but His grave and majestic message. I have just come down from the mountaintop like Moses, and I carry the law of God in my hands!"

I know a priest who, like many of us, begins his homily with the sign of the cross. But first under his breath he deliberately says, "I come," and then aloud, "in the name of the Father and of the Son and of the Holy Spirit. Amen!" Now he is in the mood. He knows that the pulpit is not a fence to straddle, but a tower from which to proclaim.

It will not matter then, who may be in the congregation. You are God's messenger. It will not matter whose gallbladder is under operation. You are the surgeon. You are there to cut if necessary, to cure if you can. You will always want to help; sometimes it may hurt. But in the scriptural sense you are no respecter of persons; you answer only to God.

Since a priest in the pulpit is the ambassador of Christ, he dare not be a Nice Nelly tossing out marshmallow flatteries because he is afraid to offend. He cannot be a perfume atomizer spraying sweet little nothings because he fears to face unpleasant themes. His goal is not popularity but preaching the Gospel. He seeks not admiration but action. When a certain popular Greek orator addressed the crowd, people used to say, "How beautifully he speaks!" But when Demosthenes spoke, they cried, "Let us march!"

Newspapers, they say, worry about the opinion of advertisers. Radio and TV programs may have to be concerned about what the sponsor may think. *Your* sponsor is Jesus Christ. We *know* what He thinks and where He stands. How sickening to hear a compromising preacher glide around moral principles like a skier around the poles on a downhill run. Such a man should be listened to only if you are standing near the rail of a ship. Nausea is inevitable.

By contrast there comes to mind the forthrightness and the

courage of a man like Wendell Phillips, who was not a preacher nor even a Catholic. His speeches are possibly out of print, but if you can get hold of a copy you will have old-time oratory at its polished and florid best. But what makes him deserve his imposing statue on Boston Common was his strange role as the hero of lost causes.

At a time when almost all about him were either yawningly indifferent or violently opposed to matters like prison reform, woman suffrage, Indian rights, Irish freedom and the abolition of slavery, Phillips dared to stand up and speak for them all. More than once he had to leave the hall under police protection. Of all the causes that he had championed, he lived to see only one succeed: when the irons of slavery were struck from the limbs of the black man. But he knows now that every one of the other "lost causes" eventually came to full flower from the green turf on his grave.

We, too, if we are to preach Christ and Him crucified, will have to preach unpopular truths. This demands not only a mite of courage but also a sturdy resolve not to be dis-couraged. In the long run we need not so much fortitude as optimism. The Curé d'Ars preached his simple sermons, and with the years saw his village change for the better before his very eyes. We preach, Sunday after Sunday, year after year, and nothing seems to happen. It is like attacking the Rockies with a nail file, or draining the Atlantic with an eyedropper. We pipe and they will not dance. We give them a tune and they will not sing.

And yet every now and then some special fruit that the pulpit shook from the tree is gathered up in the confessional. Every now and then you discover that a sermon you preached years ago, some sentences you do not remember, an incident you casually told, have had a sharp and definite effect on a man's whole life. It was you who cut the furrow and sowed the seed, but the Lord walked invisibly behind, to bless the soil and give the increase.

A confrere was recalling such an instance the other night,

though it had happened in the forties. He said he was attending the funeral of the pastor of Holy Trinity, then a national German parish, in Boston. In the vestibule he had met a gray-haired layman and they got to conversing. "This dead pastor converted me," the layman said, "and yet I never got closer to him than any of the pews are to the pulpit. During the first World War, I was a government agent. Remember how we were taught then to hate everything German? Even on the restaurant menus, sauerkraut became Liberty Cabbage. Anyway, I could speak German and I was assigned to listen to the sermons here every Sunday morning. Somebody was afraid that this pastor might be subtly sabotaging our war effort by taking sly shots at patriotism.

"I never heard one word that was unpatriotic. But Sunday after Sunday I heard a brief, clear, attractive presentation of some point of Catholic doctrine. I became more and more interested in the Catholic Church and I decided to investigate further. So I went to another rectory (I could not go to this pastor, because I was practically 'casing' him) and took a series of instructions. I was baptized and have been a Catholic ever since. The man we are burying today never knew what I have told you, but when I read about his death in the newspaper, I thought I should come to say thanks. He doesn't need it but it makes me feel better."

So we never know who is out there or what strange impact our words may have. All we do know is that the average congregation is the possible catch of fish our Savior spoke about. Pulpit rows have just as many different types of people: the devout and the indifferent, the enthusiastic and the cynical, the bright flames and the dull embers, the blue jeans and the gray flannels and possibly even the silver mink, the grimly dedicated and the just-going-through-the-motions. They are all there. The first Apostles were fishermen, and we, their spiritual descendants, should be, too. No man can predict the catch.

7 ● Department of Labor

Houdini, most elusive and incredible of escape artists, took his secrets to the grave. At least that is what the credulous like to believe. You cannot say the same of the master preachers. Read their memoirs and they all stand up in the dock to give the same testimony: there are no pulpit secrets. Success is the ancient formula of some talent and much toil.

Visit, if you will, any large theological library. Blink at the shelf upon shelf, bookcase after bookcase, the rows and rows of volumes on preaching, offering samples of sermons from the apostolic age to the atomic age. This bewilders. The "How to Preach" manuals tend to discourage. After a while you feel you are shuffling through long stretches of sawdust — it all seems so dry and dreary.

At least that was my reaction. And do you know why? I surmise I was disappointed because I did not find Ponce de Léon's fountain of youth. I wanted to discover and to pass on to others a new, mysterious, miraculous method of easy sermon writing. And it wasn't there.

When shall we learn? Learn that in anything worthwhile, from diamond mining to dentistry, there is no quick, sure, easy way. There is no substitute for plain hard work.

Thackeray is supposed to have shrugged off success by saying, "I woke up one morning and found myself famous." But some friend was so ungallant as to point out that before that blessed morn he had been writing eight hours a day for fifteen years.

One hoary old divine told a young curate, "You want to preach well? Put some sealing wax on your desk chair and stick there!" In the circumstances it would be hard to do anything else.

The Germans have an earthy phrase for the stick-to-itiveness of the diligent writer. They call it *sitzfleisch* which might be freely translated as "a plump rump that stays put."

You could make a case for sermon writing being the hardest of all writing because it deals with the elusive spiritual. How much easier it is to give a vivid picture of a supermarket or an automobile crash, compared to describing grace or salvation or eternity or heaven! You can quote, "In my Father's house are many mansions"; but you cannot lay out a blueprint or an architect's picture of the condominium. You can quote about the everlasting fires of hell, but you cannot open an asbestos briefcase and exhibit even one glowing coal. You are dealing with the supernatural, and it is not easy to make this concrete and vivid.

That is all the more reason why we should start off with the premise that if we want to preach a good sermon, it will always mean the sacrifice of time and usually the agony of hard mental work. But if we do not prepare the talk, the people will know it as surely as if we held up a huge sign saying THIS BOY SCOUT IS UNPREPARED! By the third minute he will be eligible for admittance to the Home for Little Wanderers.

Mercifully we rarely hear comments on such performances. I do recall reading one, though I don't remember just where. I suspect it was in the "Letters" column of a Catholic paper. But I never can forget the sarcasm, addressed to Sunday homilists in general.

It was more than a sharp needle. It was a deadly harpoon. With straightforward, deadpan malice the writer sought one small concession from the Sunday preacher: "Please prepare your sermon while putting on your vestments in the sacristy, instead of during your walk from the altar to the pulpit."

Sour and sardonic, of course. The milk of human kindness

curdled into tart lumps. But did he (or she) perhaps have bitter reason to write as he did?

At least you can't fault the first three words, "Prepare your sermon." I visualize a desk and a swivel chair. Behind both, a bookcase. There is where the preparation begins. Consider, first, the bookcase. If the bookcase contains mostly sermon books, the chances are that the owner does not preach exceptional sermons. If, on the other hand (and here we reprise another chapter), the shelves flash titles from history and biography and poetry, the chances are he does. Such a stable of books belongs to a broader, more adventurous mind. That some are solid spiritual volumes we take for granted. But a broad literary background provides the best equipment to produce vivid and varied and effective preaching.

Which brings to mind that in a larger library we speak of the *works* of Shakespeare and the works of Scott and the works of Dickens, precisely because they are the product of *work*. So is any first-class sermon. It may be delivered from a pulpit but it has been fashioned at a desk. The church is only the dining room where the homiletic meal is served. The desk is the hot stove in the laborious kitchen.

When a man says he does not like to preach, it often means he does not like to prepare a sermon. I doubt if the FBI and the CIA together could find a man who consistently does like the task of hammering a sermon together. Outside of lighthouse duty, writing is the loneliest job in the world. Both are solitary stints, but both, we hope, throw far a guiding beam.

Many's the time (*pace* the grammarians! Did a precisionist ever write an interesting sentence?) — well, very often — this writer has thrown a hood over his typewriter and walked down to the nearby hospital to visit the parish sick. If they are not too ill, what a reception you get! They welcome you like a cardinal or a king. They make you feel that you have made their day. They are *so* grateful.

And yet what have you actually done? The regular chaplain

has heard the confessions, and brought Communion, and perhaps anointed. All you do is listen and offer a little comfort, say a few words of encouragement, promise a prayer. But mostly you just listen. And yet their thank-yous follow you out the door. You come away feeling that you have done something worthwhile. You have helped somebody. You are appreciated, and it is a warm, wonderful sensation.

Then you go back home and sit behind that typewriter again. You stare out the window, stare down at the sheet of blank paper. Is there anything more depressing than a sheet of clean white paper? A carpenter has his hammer and nails and wood. A surgeon has his patient and his instruments. Even an undertaker has his cadaver. But the writer (and an effective preacher is usually first a writer) has nothing but a topic. Sometimes he does not even have that. His only resources are sources, and where are the good ones? Where are the fish-thrashing waters into which he can let down his net?

Most of all, he complains, he does not have the time. His day fills up with activities they never warned him about in the seminary, all the way from bazaars to bingo, from envelope salesmen to leaky ceilings and misbehaving furnaces. There are meetings of the parish council, CCD sessions, nursing homes, wakes, weddings, ushers, lectors, altar boys, sodalities, and on and on. With all this, is a man also expected to carve out, Sunday after Sunday, a Mount Rushmore of pulpit masterpieces?

It needs, of course, no ghost-come-from-the-tomb to reveal that some men are busier than others. Who was it that said that in no other profession (though I loathe the word in this connection) can you get away with doing less than in the priesthood, and in none is there more to be done if the man wants to do it! That's not the precise quotation, but that's the exact idea. A zealous priest does as much as he can, and perhaps a little more. The impossible always takes a mite longer.

One very orderly clergyman (and this is not the badge of all our tribe) had two desks in his study, with a swivel chair between them. One desk was for parish business: the bills and the collections and the bulletin and the checkbook and the rest of the sundry non-spiritual things. He could have called that desk "The Parish Chute" because on it dropped all matters parochial. The other desk was for his weekly sermon. I don't know what he called that, but if I know human nature, the swivel chair swung around much more to "The Parish Chute," and that desk wore out long before the other.

We all share a built-in tendency to put off unpleasant things. Who sprints to the dentist? And who is eager to prepare a sermon? How many homilies have been hurriedly assembled on Saturday night? While Saturday night may be ideal for dates and dances and country club dinners, just as it used to be consecrated to the weekly bath, there is no mystic aura hanging over it to make it the perfect time for sermon composition. It was pushed into that slot only because a couple of ne'er-do-wells named laziness and lack of planning shouldered it there.

Come to think of it, now that we have interpreted the Sabbath to include also the First Vespers of Sunday, with Masses being shifted to Saturday afternoon and Saturday evening, the frontiers of frenzied last-minute sermon preparation are now being pushed as far back as Saturday morning. But Saturday morning can be occupied with a funeral or a wedding or both. So, let's hear it for Friday night as the "Last Chance Saloon" for the blending of the Sunday sermon!

The opposite to all this, and a radiant ideal, is to begin preparing on Monday morning. I have known many priests who did this. I think of one who was formerly attached to the rectory where I am now living. The latter is a huge structure with a large but not up-to-date library. My room (for the last thirty-eight years) is close to the library door, and every Monday morning I would see this diligent padre pass by with an armful of books. I could recognize the *Catholic Encyclopedia*, bound volumes of the *Homiletic and Pastoral Review*, and generally a brace of other books not easily identifiable.

During the next few days, at intervals in his busy parochial schedule, Father R. would copy copious notes on the particular topic he was researching. On Sunday evening at the Holy Hour he would deliver a twenty-minute talk that held the congregation enthralled. He did not speak on Gospel themes but on some topic related to religion, like the early persecutions, or the Crusades, or religious profession, or funeral rites, or even so commonplace a subject as candles. But because he had prepared with conscientious care, and because he spoke with animation and flair, they loved it.

On the other side of the coin (why must it always be a coin? why not a greenback or the flip side of a record?) there comes to mind the different case of another confrere. He was a missionary in South America, and one night his superior abruptly informed him he was to speak the next morning at a huge outdoor Mass. The occasion corresponded to the graduation exercises at our West Point. All the dignitaries of the country, from the President down, would be there. That night he could not snare one viable thought. He said his mind was absolutely static even up to the Epistle of the Mass. But during the Epistle (since raised to the rarified rank of First Reading) he happened to glance up at the national flag, streaming out against the fierce blue tropical sky. And all at once the three colors in the flag became the three points of his talk. He stood on the platform, he spoke, he conquered.

I believe him, for he is an honorable man. I also choose to believe that behind him lay many hours of remote, unwitting preparation for just such a moment as this. I also tend to suspect that into that talk were woven swatches of previous talks, a thought gleaned from this one, and another thought adapted from that one, and all knitted together by the spirit and enthusiasm of the hour.

Did not something like this happen even to St. Anthony? At a great Ordination Mass the scheduled orator failed to appear. Prominent preachers were approached in the sacristy and asked to fill in. Each shook an eloquent head and held up defensive palms. So the superior of the Franciscans tapped Padre Antonio. After all, Antonio was only the chaplain of a monastery of Brothers high in the backwoods hills. If he fizzled, what harm? Nobody expected anything from an unknown. He could just disappear back into his original obscurity.

But, surprise! When Anthony started to speak, the air suddenly turned electric. Every shoulder leaned the slightest bit forward, every eye was riveted on the gaunt brown robe in the pulpit. He dazzled like Fourth of July fireworks. He lifted them up, held them there, gently let them down. They had never heard a man speak as this man spoke.

After the ceremony everyone wanted to know where the Franciscans had been hiding him. But Pentecostal miracle it was not. Had they but known, Anthony for ten years before had been studying the Scriptures and the Fathers of the Church in a monastery in Portugal. This occasion only broke the dam and sent the stored-up flood of his learning and fervor rushing out. That eloquence continued to pour out over all Italy till his premature death six years later.

Perversely, the memory rises of a tale they used to tell in clerical circles of an ambitious priest who used to attend every sacerdotal funeral with an all-purpose eulogy (spelled homily) tucked in his cassock, and a perennial hope in his heart that the preacher for the occasion would fail to appear. On one occasion he did not, and the young man was made, at least with the elderly bishop. His more sour-minded colleagues would have preferred that the manuscript had turned yellow in his scheming pocket.

But, as they say in some latitudes, let us not to judge. Rather pray that we may acquire the zeal and the self-discipline to decide on Monday morning what we shall talk about on the following Sunday. Then for the rest of the week, mount that topic in our brain like a magnet so that all pertinent thoughts will leap to it.

Whatever we read during the ensuing week, whomever we meet, the hospital visits we make, the letters we receive, the television shows we see, the newspaper stories we encounter — we are always alert to what they can contribute to our theme. Jot down the thoughts as they come along. These scraps will become the personal spice, sprinkled like paprika, over the more formal material lifted from more formal sources.

A well-prepared Sunday sermon often begins on Monday. A warm one has something of the preacher's own mind and heart wrapped inside.

A confrere of mine is willing to take a lie-detector test on an incident that happened as late as last month. That particular Sunday the preacher's homily had been so dismal that even his doting sister had her doubts. However, she hoped that others might have reacted differently. During the week she chanced to meet a parishioner who did not know she was the curate's sister, so she ventured to ask him if by any chance he had been to the High Mass last Sunday and what did he think of the curate's sermon? He looked her right in the eye and said, "I sent the poor man a 'Get Well' card."

One of the world's premier pianists once acidly said, "If I neglect practicing for one day, I know it. If I miss a few days, my friends can tell. If I skip two weeks, even the critics recognize it." When it comes to preaching, the dullest brain in the pews is sharp in one area. He can tell after a half dozen sentences if the man in the pulpit has prepared or not.

If we do not prepare, we rant, we repeat, we hesitate, we wander, we beat the dead horse of the obvious, we just shout louder something that everyone has heard before, as if we were a spiritual Columbus discovering a brilliant new truth. But we deceive no one. And we waste God's precious time.

8 ● Religious Illiterates?

Since some religious truths are unwelcome, we can do one of two things. We can either dilute the truth until it is watered down and made easy to swallow, or we can speak the words of truth in the tones of love, which make the truth easier to hear and accept. We must do the latter. We dare not, for fear of offending anyone, sheathe the sharp points of Christ's Gospel with velvet compromises and plush exceptions.

There are people who "love religion" if it is in terms of a sunset glow on stained-glass windows and soft organ music in the candle-lit dusk. There are others who are willing to concede that religion offers an excellent training for children, is not bad for older women and, under certain circumstances, possible even for men, provided, of course, that its precepts do not step on their business toes or cramp their swinging life-style. Such people want to hear from the pulpit only a religion of dripping sentiment and situation ethics.

In proclaiming God's truth, we are supposed to suit the sermon to the audience, but this gives us leeway only with the pattern, never with the cloth. Most of us rarely get a congregation of all soldiers or all nurses or all divorcées. Sometimes the audience is so blended it baffles you. In my present rectory, we used to take turns every six weeks or so at preaching in the huge chapel behind the high red-brick walls of the old House of the Good Shepherd. Here, if ever, was an assorted assembly.

In the front pews sat a score of Good Shepherd Nuns in their gleaming white habits. Behind them knelt a couple of rows of

"Magdalens" in robes of somber black. (The Magdalens are an order of penitents who have turned from a life of sin to lead an even stricter life than the Good Shepherd Nuns themselves. We always heard that among them were a few heroic souls who had never strayed, but who had joined the penitents out of deep humility. So you never knew; it was like the firing squad where one of the rifles had a blank cartridge.)

All around the chapel hung two huge galleries. On one side knelt the "Preservatives," so called because they were teen-agers who had not yet gone wrong, but who, because of bad home environment, easily might. On the other side of the gallery slouched the ladies of the evening, sentenced to the institution by the court. Courtesans, if you will.

What kind of broad-umbrella sermon do you preach to cover all these? We agreed that the best bet was the all-inclusive fundamentals like faith or salvation or Christian hope or God's love for us all, and our duty to love one another. Even then, some of them might misinterpret "love." You had to build a rainbow arch that would stretch from the apostolic to the alcoholic.

Monsignor Robert Hugh Benson (whose father was the archbishop of Canterbury) claimed he knew a priest who had a double assignment. Each Sunday morning he had to say Mass for a group of convicts in the nearby jail, and each Sunday afternoon he had to give a Holy Hour for some cloistered nuns. To each congregation, he gave the same talk. Maybe he reasoned that they were all "shut-ins."

So, though the homiletic books always urge us to tailor our talks to the audience, the ordinary priest in the ordinary town rarely gets a congregation of merely "farmers" or "students" or "policemen." He just has "people." This is not to denigrate the faces that look up at you from the pews. There was a time, I am afraid, when in more senses than one, the preacher in the pulpit tended to look down upon the congregation. Those were the days when the clergyman was one of the few educated men in the place. This situation held in many little villages all the way from old Ireland to New England, and from French Canada to Bavaria and Sicily. At the turn of the century going to high school was the exception rather than the rule. The clergyman, be he priest or minister, while not exactly a scholar among illiterates, or an intellectual Sequoia among shrubs, was certainly several cuts above his congregation in educational background.

It is not hard to imagine that in those circumstances some preachers disdainfully tossed their pearls to the unwashed and unappreciative herd. Like pompous Poobahs, they could pontificate in a kind of ecclesiastical snobbery, because they had read a few books. One such cleric, in order to impress his rustic flock, used to toss in a multi-jointed word every now and then, like "Armageddon" or "Mesopotamia," whether the words fitted or not, so that nobody would forget who was the intellectual among them.

To say that things are different now is like hanging a wreath around the obvious. As someone said of the average congregation, "How can you expect them to be sheep, when so many of them have sheepskins?" No longer dare the preacher be condescending or patronizing; he must present his case to equals.

Still, there is one corner of the picture that should not be overlooked. Educated the congregation may be, on a general academic level, but this does not mean they need no religious instruction. Their sleeves may wear all kinds of bright, collegiate chevrons, and the group together may boast more degrees than a thermometer, but their knowledge of matters religious can be almost microscopic. I still cling to a stubborn conviction (developed by stubbing my toe on sundry examples) that a man can be a first-class surgeon or a topflight lawyer or a high-ranking architect, and still be little more than a kindergarten Catholic.

How many professional men could explain promptly and lucidly the difference between the Immaculate Conception and the Virgin Birth? Once, of course, they knew precisely. But religious information is like any other kind of information; it melts under the quiet heat of passive neglect. Once we knew (shades of the seventh grade and drill-sergeant Sister Eduardo!) the boundaries of Brazil, the source of the Nile, the capital of Mozambique. Would any of us like to face a quiz on these now? But time rusts knowledge as well as nails. Unused muscles can atrophy. If we do not use facts, the chances are we soon forget them.

At the same time, it is depressing to realize that while the congregation may have only a thimbleful of knowledge about its Faith, it has oceans of information about current goings-on. They know much more about Grace Kelly than about sanctifying grace, more about money orders than about Holy Orders, more about the gas bill than the Gospel. It is even possible, if you inquire, that one or the other among them may be under the impression that an Epistle is the wife of an Apostle, and that an indulgence is something you take Alka-Seltzer for. It is not unheard of that an Act of Contrition conclude, "and to end my life. Amen." I recall having been asked to arrange a "Solid High Mass" in that ancient era when we had Solemn High Masses. Which makes me wonder nostalgically, whatever became of all those dalmatics and tunics?

The truth is that most Catholics learned their catechism as children and by rote. It never went through a thinking man's filter. Much of it gradually evaporated with the mists of the years. Part of the preacher's task is to provide a continuing refresher course. His mission is to inform the uninformed, and to inspire the informed, because knowledge alone, God knows, is not enough.

Many years ago, a little group of us would take our places almost every afternoon at the Congressional Library in Washington. Most were working on some kind of thesis. The atmosphere had the quiet of a cathedral sanctuary, broken only by the turning of pages and the scratching of the old-style fountain pens. It was Academics Anonymous, a convention of lighthouses.

Then one fine day, two conservatively dressed men walked in, tapped one of the researchers on the shoulder, and escorted him out. We saw in the newspaper the next day that he was a long-sought counterfeiter, brushing up on his steel engraving there in the Congressional Library at the U.S. Government's expense.

Now, this man certainly had knowledge, especially in his particular field. He had industry, because he was reading no light novel but a very technical textbook. But he did not have much conscience or character or moral conviction. The other kind of conviction he would acquire soon enough. It all demonstrates that along with information you need integrity. And it is a prime purpose of the pulpit to provide the one and to plead for the other.

9 ● View from the Pew

It is a charming fiction, solicitously nourished by those who know nothing about it, that the man in the pulpit "has it made," because before him sits a ready-made, captive audience. Granted they are there, but realism has to take its scalpel and cut a sharp distinction. (Our theology professor used to say with a wry smile, "Seldom admit. Never deny. Always distinguish.")

So here is the distinction. If by "captive" one means that there are a certain number of bodies out there ranged in long rows who will probably never jump up crying, "Objection!" or never walk out in protest, I concede. But if anyone thinks that these same people have flung out a red carpet so that you can comfortably and gracefully walk into their minds, I deny. No babble-onian captivity here!

The congregation is not there, shoulders tilted forward expectantly, as if you were a teacher confiding the topics about which you are going to question them in an upcoming exam. They are not listening for the number that wins the state lottery. They are just there. They are not probably thinking about anything religious at all. Their thoughts, if you could poll them, range over a thousand other things, from just what causes the rattle they noticed that morning in the car, to wondering how long it will take to get an appointment with an eye doctor.

Only the carcass is there; the mind may be anywhere. You have to flag down their attention. They will be interested, only if you are interesting. Mere platitudes, dull obviosities, boring repetitions, will drift past their clean ears like pigeons coasting past the steeple of a church. True, they will always be dimly aware of the preacher's voice, a kind of remote roar like a passing plane. But to what avail if the plane does not land and unload its cargo?

The man looking at a dull movie can yawn and leave. Up to now, a similar procedure is frowned upon in better churches. The man listening to a sermon on the radio can shake his head and twist the dial, and by that gesture pinch the preacher by the ear and fling him far out into kilocycle space. But the man squirming under a droning, stolid pulpit is the prisoner of convention. He can only sink down into the anesthesia of sleepy-eyed boredom. He is there and he is not. His brain is in neutral.

So you see there is really no such thing as a captive audience. There is only an open-door opportunity. And you should know what you may be walking into.

THE AUDIENCE . . . ITS CONCERNS

Quite recently I preached a Marian Week or a kind of mininovena in a charming town in one of the Maritime Provinces which had been turned into a mini-paradise by gorgeous June weather. Beyond the glassy waters, the rest of the world might be hurrying along at a hyped-up pace and twitching from headline jitters, but here life had slowed to a serene stroll. That week the front page of the local paper had featured the photo of a sweet old lady whose skillful needle had made her the area's "Patch Quilt Queen."

On the last night, there was a parish dance in the adjoining hall. Fiddles scraped, accordions wheezed, colored streamers swayed in the soft, summery breeze. Gliding dancers nodded and smiled in what seemed a dreamworld of radiant pleasure and perfect joy.

On the sidelines the local judge leaned over to me and whispered, "You see how happy these people are? Well, let me tell you something. I grew up among them. Later, as a lawyer, I had them for clients. Practically every one of them has some secret sorrow, some thorny problem, some dark shadow on his life.

When you preach to people, keep that in mind. They need comfort, courage, hope."

It brought back a passage I had read in Emerson long ago (and I quote from a memory that certainly is not bonded) which goes something like this: "Under your pulpit may be sitting the shoemaker whose wife has just gone mad; the spinster who has just been insulted by her neighbor and who still carries the splinter in her heart; the blacksmith who knows that he has jaundice and fears that he will never be well again. These are the people you are preaching to. Speak to them kindly."

We can update that to the mother who has just found out that her oldest boy is using drugs, or the father whose coveted promotion to a higher desk has just been blocked by cheap office politics, or the family whose darling youngest has just been diagnosed as a severe diabetic.

Clichés, though trite and dull, are usually true, and none is truer than, "You never know." From where we look in the pulpit things are not always what they seem. That elegant cashmere coat in the front pew which seems the very symbol of conceited success may be buttoned over a broken heart. The mother whose head drops to sleep during your brilliant peroration may have been up all night with a sick child. The old fellow who alternately sucks his lips in and then pushes them out, while you are so lucidly explaining the Trinity, may be only getting used to a new double-decker of uncomfortable dentures.

The more we mingle with people and learn at least a little of their personal lives, the more compassion we are bound to feel. What a crime and a blunder then (Talleyrand rated the latter worse than the former), if we ever sink to sarcasm or resort to blistering abuse! Sin, of course, we must condemn, the sinner never. So easy it is, in a pulpit monologue, to win an argument and to lose a soul. Every sermon should be played in the key of sympathy.

Though it is probably apocryphal, I always liked that story about Father Damien making his morning tea. He is supposed to have spilled some of the boiling water on the bare toes of his sandaled foot. Instinctively he winced and cried out. Then he realized he had felt no pain. The next Sunday morning he looked out at his congregation and began, "We lepers . . ."

This is rapport with an audience, raised to Alpine heights. But at least each of us can try to put himself on a level with his hearers, and never give the impression that he is addressing them from the lofty minaret of perfection, and has nothing in common with those poor sinners down there in the pews. Better if we project the attitude that we are all passengers on the same liner, subject to the same monotony, the same storms, the same seasickness.

Our Lord had a way of letting the people know he was thinking on their wavelength: "What *man among you* does not let his ox or his ass out of the stall on the Sabbath to water it?" "Suppose *one of you* has a hundred sheep . . ." "If *one of you* has a son . . . who falls into a pit . . ." "When the Lord saw her, his heart was touched . . ."

And so would be ours, did we only know the troubles of our flock. Or do we know, and fail to make allowances?

THE AUDIENCE . . . ITS ENVIRONMENT

A rectory should be like God's embassy in a foreign country, a tiny spiritual island in a vast secular sea. On its walls hang holy pictures and crucifixes. In its bookcases stand rows of theological works. On its tables lie all sorts of Catholic magazines. The talk at dinner may be about the Red Sox or the Yankees or the Cowboys or the Colts, but it is also about sick calls and sodalities and census and CCD and Nuptial Masses and the bishop and the transfers of curates and the chancery and so on. Take the house as a whole, the milieu (to borrow the current jargon) is mainly spiritual, religious, ecclesiastical. Life revolves on the axis of God and the Church.

But the Catholics in the Sunday morning pews live for the most part in a very different kind of world. Some of the sociologists call it neopaganism, which means that it is the paganism of old Rome, only that the togas are now topcoats, and the chariots are Chevys, and the privy has become indoor plumbing. All around the Catholic in the street swirls the new and almost universal permissiveness; the deadly marsh-mist of pornography; the invisible but deadly fallout of "Do your own thing!"; the junking of moral standards; the spread of a drug culture that the old pagans never knew; the "So what?" acceptance of co-ed dorms; the blasé tolerance of wife-swapping; the incredible open cult of homosexuality. Move over, Sodom! Take a back seat, Gomorrah!

This is the atmosphere in which the average Catholic in the street lives. In it he moves and has his being. Where else can he go? Perhaps the last thing that catches his eye before he comes through the church door on Sunday morning is the row of billboards (those stained-glass windows in the cathedral of commerce) featuring scantily clad and voluptuous figures, waiting there like the tempting meat in a bare-trap. After Mass, when he drops into the drugstore, his eyes will fall on rows and rows of raunchy paperbacks. The Sunday paper he tosses into his car carries lurid stories whose shameless details it would be unthinkable to print a few years back. That evening when he turns on the television, out of the tube may ooze material more suited to a stable than to a living room. We are rapidly approaching the era of the comedian who could use Sani-Flush as a gargle.

To counteract all this is the awesome job of the Sunday Mass homily. What else is there to do it? If you want a motive to work hard on your Sunday sermon, just realize that for many out there it is the only antidote for a whole week's poison. Who else speaks up for God and morality? Who else reminds the average Catholic in the street of his obligations and his ideals?

It would be nice if God got equal time, but He never does and never will. That is why those ten minutes that He does get from the Sunday morning pulpit are important out of all proportion to their length. That is why we should try to make that sermon worthwhile. It is a last resort. In a workaday, pleasure-oriented world, it is God's only chance at rebuttal.

The preacher trying to neutralize the effect of secular society is pulling against wind and tide. To make that sermon something that people will listen to and heed, takes bending at the oars till the back aches and the hands blister. Not literally, of course, but in its own way preparing a good sermon can be just as hard.

Maybe for our comfort it may sometimes help to remember that one of the early American bishops took for his motto, *"Quies in Coelo,"* a kind of prodding reminder that for the present it has to be *"Labor in Terra."* Rest is for eternity, but from here to eternity it is work. And anyone who thinks that turning out a fairly decent sermon is not work, has never tried to produce one.

THE AUDIENCE . . . ITS COMPOSITION

Luther was honest enough to admit that when he saw some famous person in his congregation, he was strongly tempted to address and impress that particular personality. Most of us will probably not have prominent people coming to hear us, so this particular temptation (like arson and idolatry) will never give us much trouble. Our target should be the average man. Some preachers take this literally and select some unknown individual in one of the rear pews, and direct their words specifically at him. They claim that this helps them to give their sermon a warmer, more personal, more intimate, more conversational tone.

Personally, it is a method I could not handle. First, it might be embarrassing to the individual singled out, and secondly, it certainly would be a distraction to me. When I preach, I would rather not see anyone in particular. All the books emphasize eye contact, but unless they mean that your eyes sweep across the whole audience like a searchlight ranging the sky, I can see where it could present drawbacks. I might find myself wondering where have I seen that fellow's face before, or is that woman really wearing an auburn wig? But it is a decision for the individual. *"Suum cuique!"* To each his own choice! (For the purists, maybe that is not the accurate interpretation. I remember seeing the Latin on a Hussar's helmet once, and the gory implication seemed to be, "Give each enemy what he deserves!" Probably blessed by the regimental chaplain, too.)

So that the voice projects better, most speakers, I think, prefer to fix their eyes on the anonymous rear rows. Because they are back there like a kind of vague blur, it should make us realize that they are ordinary, run-of-the-mill people. This should remind us that we are not addressing erudite theologians or ascetical mystics. We are talking to minds that need instruction and hearts that need comfort. You can't go wrong with a blend of information and consolation.

Perhaps I am unduly pessimistic, but I am not sure that the average Catholic is too clear about some of the terms we toss off so glibly, like Gethsemane and Golgotha and Pentecost and even Nazareth. Bethlehem, thanks to ten thousand Christmas carols, he surely knows.

There probably will be, too, in the usual Sunday congregation a sprinkling of young people (those who still go to church) who look upon the preacher coldly if for no other reason but that he is an authority-figure (in their jargon) and so represents "the establishment" for which read "enemy." They resent a situation wherein the man in the pulpit promulgates doctrines and decrees, and offers no opportunity for discussion or denial.

Such a youth is, of course, eons away from his grandfather, who, when something "was given off the altar" accepted it like the law of gravity. But those days, and even the more recent ones of "Sister says," have become rare theological antiques. Not that you can do much about it. But you should be forewarned that every congregation probably has a few scowling young-uns who are sitting there not merely passive, but, in the spirit of their rebellious day, even hostile. On their banners fly the slogan, "Whatever is, is wrong." It is not entirely their fault. They are victims of the secular and irreligious atmosphere all about them. But if we present the cause of Christ lucidly and vividly and attractively, even they will listen.

There are two other types of listeners you can expect to find in any substantial audience, and a third kind that, with a little bit of luck, you may encounter. Type one is the strainer. He or she is like that old wire-mesh kitchen gadget used to trap coffee grounds, orange seeds and the like. It lets the good things go through and perversely hangs on to the trivia, the scraps. So we have human strainers who will catch and hold on to your every mispronunciation, your grammatical error, your inexact quotation, your wrong date; in a word, any mistake that you may possibly make. But the heart and soul of your sermon, the core of your message, flows right through such picayune minds leaving no good whatever. Characters like these are about as welcome as ants at a picnic. Try to forgive them and forget them. They may not let you forget, but try anyway.

Then there are the watering cans. They receive the message, all right, but they never dream it was meant for them. Like a watering can, they hold the homily over the head of someone else and smugly think, "Isn't so-and-so getting hers this morning!"

The ideal listener (and pray they crowd your pews) is neither the strainer nor the watering can but the thermos bottle. They know that the sermon really begins only when the preacher stops. When he says "Amen," their spirit of faith says, "OK. Let's go!" So they retain the essence of the talk as it was poured out, whether cold logic or warm appeal, and take it home with them so that now and then during the week they can take a thoughtful, reinvigorating sip. Of such is the kingdom of homiletics!

10 ● The Works Inside the Watch

If anyone should ask me (an extremely unlikely hypothesis) what is the very first thing I do in writing a sermon, I should in all honesty reply that I stare out the window, pace the floor, bite my lip, suck on a pencil and look around for something else to do that will put off the sermon writing for at least a little longer. But if someone with a district-attorney cast of mind bluntly asks what is the first thing I *should* do (and occasionally even do) the answer would have to be: I go to headquarters and ask the help of God; I drop down on my knees and pray.

After all, if I am going to talk *about* God, should I not first talk *to* Him? So, the first step in preparing a sermon ought to be an earnest, humble, manly prayer. You lower your bucket and beg the Lord to fill it.

When we were graduated from Our Lady of Perpetual Help Grade School in Brooklyn (way back during the prehistoric days of World War I) we had pinned on the lapels of our blue serge suits (with the billowing knickerbockers and the long black stockings and the button shoes) a neat blue-and-white enameled pin with the motto, *"Auxilium Ab Alto"* (or "Help from on High"). Incidentally, back in those medieval days, in the second half of the eighth grade we were taught the elements of Latin and of algebra. There was no nonsense then, and we could spell and parse, and the teacher ruled the class.

Anyway, I never forgot what was drummed into us: that we would always need that "Help from on High," and as the years roll on, I have come to believe that one needs it most of all in try-

71

ing to compose a sermon. Where else can you really find that help? Ask the man who has tried to find it in books about preaching, like this.

For some weird reason, there now rises up before me, plain as Banquo's accusing ghost at the banquet, the memory of a man wearing a white glove, Ireland's Daniel O'Connell. Because he had accepted a challenge to a duel when he was a hotheaded young man, and in the encounter had slain his opponent, Daniel O'Connell never approached the altar rail for Communion but that his bloodguilty hand was gloved in penitent white. And, more often than not, a rosary was nestled in that white glove. But his hand cradled the beads at other times, too.

One day when O'Connell was pacing back and forth in a corridor of the House of Commons, a fellow Irishman came bursting out of the chamber and spied him. "Glory be to God, O'Connell!" he exclaimed. "What are you doing out here? Don't you know that in a little while your country's fate will be decided in there?" O'Connell unclasped the hands folded behind his back, and disclosed a little string of black beads. "Maybe I am doing more for Ireland out here," he said, "than all the rest of you in there. Soon I shall go in there and make my speech, but I am asking the Mother of God to put the words on my lips!" And she did, because O'Connell became known throughout Ireland as the Great Liberator.

The reasoning for prayer behind preaching is not complex. It is simplicity itself. Before we stand in the pulpit to speak, we should first sit at our desk to write. But before we sit at our desk to write, we should get down on our knees to pray. A sermon is a spiritual motor and as such needs the spiritual fuel of God's grace. The gas pump is prayer.

They call a clergyman a man of the cloth. The older designation was better: a man of God. Thomas Carlyle, that sour, dour, dyspeptic Scotchman, once acidly said about his pastor, "What this parish needs is a man who knows God other than by hearsay."

72

Edgar Guest, who could not hold Carlyle's pen wiper as a writer, and who was annually voted by Harvard undergraduates as the world's worst poet, still said something right on target when he wrote, "I would rather *see* a sermon than *hear* one." Should not a priest be almost like a church steeple that, just by being in the midst of men, quietly reminds them of God?

Even pagan old Aristotle was unconsciously strumming the same string when he wrote, "The character of the speaker is his most powerful weapon of persuasion."

The horrible opposite was best phrased by one who was certainly no ascetic, King Louis the Great. After a celebrated court preacher had finished a thundering sermon on eternity, the monarch said to him at the church doors, "Monseigneur, when I hear your words, I am terrified. But when I see your life, I am reassured."

A pulpit hypocrite is like a water skier. He skims flashily over the surface, but he has no depth and he delivers no cargo. Scandals in the sanctuary and defections from the priesthood have sadly altered the view from the pew. In these uncertain days more people tend to look up at the pulpit with the raised eyebrows of suspicion. In the back of the congregation's collective mind may easily rise the thought, as they hear self-control praised and sin blasted, "After all, he has to say that. He is supposed to say it. But does he believe it? And does he live up to it himself?"

Perhaps their thoughts hark back to the television commercial they saw the previous night, when the football hero poised the bottle of Lovely Lilac Deodorant at just the proper angle and sprayed forth its glowing qualities. And as they watched, they were thinking, way back in the mezzanine of their brain, "He gets paid to say all this. But I wonder: Does he really think so? And does he actually use the stuff himself?"

Is it rash judgment to think that the faces looking up from the church benches sometimes wonder the same thing about us? Do we really use our product, the Gospel, the Commandments of

God, or do we just advertise all these? Do we really spend our lives in the house of God, or do we merely conduct a professional guided tour on Sunday mornings? Do we practice our Faith, or just peddle it?

You don't have to be a saint. You do have to be sincere. A priestly life that is always striving to be what it should be is the best *remote* preparation for any sermon. Humble, pleading prayer is the best *immediate* preparation. The priest who does not pray is the self-assured Pharisee who thinks he can do it alone. This is the Matterhorn of egotism. It is also the ocean floor of folly. Deliver us, O Lord!

11 ● Sermon Books

A priest I know quite well, who had preached for some years over the radio, was advised by the late Cardinal Cushing to compile a volume of his sermons and publish them. For a couple of years he managed to convey to his well-meaning Eminence a string of silky excuses, till one day on the occasion of Confirmation the cardinal practically put the point of his crozier at the priest's throat and, with twinkling eyes, demanded, "Are you going to publish, or not?"

The flustered priest, unwilling to have his Adam's apple transformed into instant cider, between gasps promised that he would. It was publish or perish. So, not long afterward, he came out with a book of sermons whose preface was titled, "For Young Priests Only," on the prudent assumption that it would be extremely rash to counsel one's crusty contemporaries.

The opening sentence of that preface was disarming. It said, "All sermon books are terrible, including this one. All right, especially this one." The last time I saw the author he confided that, with the usual unusual exceptions, he had found no reason to alter his opinion.

Perhaps you have been more fortunate, and your experience has been different, in which bit of serendipity (the unexpected encounter with the pleasant) I congratulate you. However, most of the padres who collegially gripe with me, nod melancholy assent to the rarity of really good sermon collections. I have bought very few, and do not intend to list any, because tastes in this area differ radically. Still, having leafed through literally dozens of sermon books in our Boston theological libraries, I cannot truthfully enthuse over many. As a matter of sour fact, I am tempted to hope that if there is a special purgatory for dull, droning preachers who torture the patience of innocent congregations, it might fittingly take the form of confinement in a huge homiletic hall, condemned there to read every sermon collection and not skip one flat, gray sentence. But surely the Lord is too merciful for that!

Still, even the driest and most pedestrian compilation of sermons yields its own surprising and shining benefit. It is this: After you have trudged through endless paragraphs of flat boredom, where is the man who does not murmur, "Bourdaloue or Bossuet or Sheen I may not be, but at least I can come up with something as good as that!" And thus, in the devious ways of Divine Providence, these stolid, heavy pages have contributed their own unsuspected by-product: they have primed the pump of a man's honest pride. They whisper, "You can do it. Roll your own!"

Undoubtedly there are many things that one man can borrow from another, and the fit does not greatly matter, like an umbrella or a shoehorn. But there are other things where the fit is most important, like a pair of shoes or a shirt or a suit. In this class falls the sermon, for the chances are that the sleeves may be too long, or the shoulders too tight, or, "Sam, you made the pants too long!"

The sermon we lift from another's book was *his* sermon, the product of *his* brain, and tuned to the beat of *his* heart. The congregation wants *your* sermon, as much a part of you as your breath or your pulse. It is one thing to scoop up an idea here or there from another man's talk, but quite another to kidnap his whole text. It just does not work.

Borrow, if you will, the other fellow's toothpaste, but, please, not his toothbrush. Doesn't the very idea make you feel queasy? To memorize and deliver somebody else's speech — is it not literally like taking the words out of his mouth?

A printed sermon is like a lake. You skim across it, and if you are lucky, you take a fish here, perhaps another there. But you take only the occasional fish. You leave the lake behind. In other words you should read a sermon with your pencil poised like a fishing pole. When you see the ripple of a bright idea, or when you feel the impact of something striking (perish the pun!), you swish that out, and you drop your line into the next page. There you may find something as unappealing as a rusty bedspring. But a few pages on may yield another panting, shimmering beauty.

(Perhaps it should be noted here that I am speaking of that harmless clerical kleptomania, that almost taken-for-granted sermon shoplifting, which confines its pious larceny to use in a local Sunday sermon or in an obscure parish novena. That is why some of us publish sermons: not that we think they are oratorical masterpieces, but in the hope that they may provide some material or ideas for fellow priests who have far less time for writing talks. But it certainly is not kosher to take another man's sermon — or a great part of it — and *publish* it as your own, or send it out *over the air*. That, brother, does not seem to be quite just. But it is done. I could show you wounds.)

There is nothing more pathetic than playing Little Sir Echo to someone else's sermon. I would much rather listen to any ordinary priest (like myself, if you press me) fumbling and stumbling along in his own earnest way than hear a pitiful plastic imitation of someone like Archbishop Sheen. Such a performance usually comes off like a symphony attempted on a kazoo. Or Beethoven on bongo drums. It just doesn't ring true.

Perhaps it is because I have been guilty of several myself, that I reluctantly concede that the average sermon book is Dullsville on the Dry. Rather recently my heart leaped up (though no rainbow was in the sky) when I learned from the jacket of a new sermon book that it had been written in a German abbey famous for its three-story wine cellar. Alas, as you read along, you knew that these pages must have been written in a very remote wing. You looked in vain for one sparkling bubble.

By and large the average published sermon runs on far too long for practical use. Do not censor the author too heavily for this. He is merely following the tradition of ages. For some curious reason printed sermons are supposed to be long. The writer, as it were, graciously escorts you through an extensive orchard. It is up to you to pause where you will, and pluck the fruit that appeals. The sermon is wholesale; the reader is retail.

You may not believe it, but the blurb of one modern sermon book enthusiastically invited the preacher to supply his own examples and illustrations. This has to be the very Mount Everest of salesmanship. Are not the examples and the illustrations precisely what the ordinary harassed preacher seeks? The doctrine he presumably knows. What he desperately wants is the "for instances," the vivid parade of illuminating examples or perfect illustrations to clinch his point. This particular book with incredible chutzpah paternally suggests that you supply these yourself. It helps you understand just how Tom Sawyer got that fence painted.

Homily services offer the closest approach to a prefabricated sermon, architected for a particular Sunday. Some day science may come along with a compressed tablet called "Instant Pulpit." On Saturday you just pop one into your mouth, pick up your pen, and let the adjectives fall where they may. Someday, but not yet, and don't hold your breath. This discovery will probably hit the market after the Anti-Temptation Roman Collar, which will kill temptations the way a chemical dog collar kills fleas.

While these paragraphs have been a little less than enthusiastic about sermon books, this might be the proper place to put in a plug (as Addison or Thackeray might not phrase it) for books in general. Among the elders of a certain religious community, there survives the legend of the grizzled old missionary who had just concluded the annual ten-day retreat to a group of nuns in the days way back when. Mother Superior (and as a rule

these lofty ladies have more diplomacy in their wimple than am-
bassadors have in their whole embassies) made the tactless mistake of asking the retreat master whether he would prefer, as a
grateful gift from the Sisters, a box of cigars or a book. "Sister,"
said the missionary, "I already have a book."

Admittedly there are some priests who seem almost to take
pride in being anti-intellectual. Their birettas should be hard
hats, except that now there are no birettas. Such men often work
diligently in the parish. They build up parish bands, bingos, sodalities, CYO's — everything but their own intellectual development.

But isn't this a personal tragedy? Is it not a pity to have
received a reasonably broad education, touching all the points of
the cultural compass from philosophy to history to theology to
Scripture to Canon Law and sundry other disciplines, and then to
leave that mental field lie fallow, and plant nothing after ordination morning? Is it not a criminal waste of such a background to
read nothing more demanding than *Newsweek* or *Sports Illustrated*? Isn't it like a surgeon who would use his scalpel to slice
a snack of midnight cheese?

How can it happen? Simply, because in the priesthood, if we
live it sincerely, there is no sanction (no reward, no punishment)
except the spiritual. From one point of view it is a calling where
a man can never do enough. But on the other hand there is no
field of life where a man can get away with doing less.

If a doctor wants to cure patients, he has to read up on medicine every week of the year. If a lawyer wants to win cases, he
has to keep up with the decisions of the courts and go deep and
often into the books. A successful engineer has to keep abreast
with new materials and new methods.

A priest, on the contrary, can survive with minimal application. Whether he wishes to "read up" or not, depends solely on
his individual decision. In the confessional he does not need penitents in order to survive, the way a doctor does need patients. If
his sermons are poor, he hears no boos and he experiences no

boycott, and suffers no loss of personal income. He has to do his best *for God*, or he will not do it at all.

At this moment the brightest names on the theological marquees are Rahner and Küng and Schillebeeckx and Teilhard de Chardin and Häring and Congar and Lubac — but the list is long. They are all famous, but my slow brain finds much in their writings that is foggy. Often they lose me. Sometimes in modern Catholic authors I get the impression of scholarship walking the tightrope of near-heresy. However, whether we are attracted to the new developments in theology or not, as priests of our times we have the obligation to be familiar with the current literature. We have, please God, our firm orthodox anchorage, and a theological Pied Piper can lead off only intellectual children.

But beyond the modern theologians and the clerical trade journals, the man who would write a fair sermon needs good secular reading, too — if only to absorb a better style and an easier way with words. Here the old rule still holds: of the best books read those that appeal to you. Why waste valuable time and a trained mind on trivia or trash? One of the high tragedies of our time is that so many lordly trees are felled to be fed into tripe-writers and eventually turned into scurvy paperbacks.

Mission Fathers, occupying an absent curate's quarters during the parish mission, sometimes claim they can tell a good deal about him from his medicine cabinet: whether he was a hypochondriac with scores of medicine bottles and pill capsules, or whether he was a dandy with a lavish lineup of lotions and colognes. By the same token you can run your eyes over the volumes in his bookcase and almost fluoroscope his mind. If you find there not just sermon books, but some classics of literature, a sprinkling of biography, an anthology or two of poetry, one or the other book of history, then you know that here lives a *soggarth* who is nourishing the whole man. He has at his disposal a mental menu with all the necessary vitamins. If he is serious about his own soul, the solidly spiritual will be there, too. This we take for granted. And from such a well-rounded cleric (with no reference to personal architecture — this can be either gauntly Gothic or plumply Romanesque) should come attractive and stimulating homilies.

Do I hear in the background the sullen, rising roar of mutiny, the surly protest, "Who has time for all this?" Protest acknowledged and recorded. I am merely trying to say in an indirect way: in your reading don't waste your time on junk. Many of us do, you know.

Poor old Gutenberg might groan at the ill use to which his movable block letters have been put through the ages. Curiously, it was not too long after Gutenberg that the most widely reprinted of all sermon books began to blanket the pastoral market. In that century it ran through ninety editions. It was called, *"Dormi Secure!"* or, in a liberal translation, "Sleep in peace!" The author had reference to a good conscience, but would it not also be the perfect epitaph for many a sermon book?

There are undoubtedly some superb collections of pulpit gems. But we keep our secrets, don't we? Or, did you ever try recommending a restaurant?

12 ● Deepfreeze

The preacher's Fort Knox — that is what a filing system is. More than invaluable, it is almost indispensable. We all read. We are impressed by certain facts or figures or ideas or illustrations. But we forget. Like flowered patterns on a frosty windowpane, what once charmed or fascinated us, vanishes. But with a filing system you can store it all in a safe-deposit vault. The click of a camera holds the foam-crested wave forever, and the click of a clipping scissors can hold forever an interesting item that otherwise would have perished.

More than one effective sermon has been written with a pair of scissors. I know a priest who, when he was young, was forever cutting out pieces from newspapers and magazines. I suspect he still is. In those days he was tall and thin, so we irreverently dubbed him "The Lanky Clipper," feeling that Joe DiMaggio would not mind.

But it was not merely the cut-up part of his character that intrigued us; it was what the squirrel did with all those hoarded nuts. He did not bury them. He arranged them in his filing cabinet. You could go to him, if you were pressed, and ask him if he had any material on anything from abortion to judgment, or from Luther to Zacchaeus, and his long tapering fingers would riffle through the manila folders like a harpist flitting over silver strings, and he would smilingly hand you paragraphs, pages, articles.

Obviously the towering advantage of having such a file yourself is that you always have at least kindling wood to start your sermon fire. You have stock on the stove, always in readiness for the next pot of homiletic soup. But notice this. Our friend, "The Lanky Clipper," did not start clipping during this week for next Sunday's sermon. It was always a long-range deal. He did his reading and his clipping with all future sermons in mind. "Will this help me sometime? Then I'll file it." He read and clipped and filed for all possible tomorrows.

Now, here is the danger. Priests who start filing, like most enthusiastic beginners, often go overboard. They clip and file all kinds of junk. Well perhaps better do this than never file at all, for at least you will have begun. But after a while you will save your predatory scissors or your pirating fingers for the really colorful quote, the truly stabbing statistic, the genuinely apt illustration, the rarely heard anecdote.

If I opened the drawer a foot away from this typewriter and showed you my own file, I would not blame you for looking down a scornful nose and shaking a sympathetic head. You might airily dismiss it as looking like the wrath of God, an indictment I hope never to be able to verify. All I actually have is a couple of old shoeboxes, and if shoeboxes ever get dropsy, these are swollen enough to be in the last stages. Crammed into the shoeboxes are rows of small, shaggy envelopes, most of them cornered with the old-fashioned pink two-cent stamp of the 1920s.

Many of these old envelopes are from the letters my mother sent me during the six years when I was in the seminary. For me they have always had a sentimental attachment, the light that still pours down from the long since burnt-out star. But as a matter of cold practicality, I advise, if *you* are starting a file, to invest in some large typing-paper-size manila folders. In our seminary days we would not dream of asking for such a luxury. In that Spartan time we "made do" with what we had. Even when we had to go to town to see the doctor, most of us had to borrow a rabat and Roman collar. We majored in survival and minored in theology. And we were incredibly happy.

For sheer delight no one has ever put clipping and filing in the same class as skiing down an Alpine slope or lofting a crisp five iron to a postage-stamp green. To be frank, it is an unmitigated nuisance. It is one thing to read the article or the item and to appreciate it, but it is quite another to go to the trouble of scissoring it and dropping it into its proper alphabetical slot. This, more often than not, becomes plain drudgery.

Many begin, but few continue. The seed is planted but it falls among the thorns of laziness and lack of self-discipline. Filing takes a little time and some trouble and a bit of patience and much perseverance. It is something like brushing your teeth: there is no attraction to it and no glamor in it, but it pays off.

That annoying need of routine brushing preserves those bicuspids and postpones the day when some dentist will have to say, "Well, there's your shiny new bridge. Now come across!" In the same way, the habit of filing away articles will make you happy on that day when you get a sudden request to speak and have very little time to prepare. With a fair filing system you have been preparing for just such an emergency. Now all you need do is arrange and digest the material already assembled. You will be happily surprised at the savory and nourishing meal you can whip up from the victuals in the file's deepfreeze.

Along with the file might go what you could call a pulpit diary. This does not mean a day-to-day account of your life, a la Pepys or Boswell. How many people begin diaries (like filing systems) and leave off in late January? Some men get rich on unused pages of diaries as other men get rich on the mustard left on dinner plates. For most of us a daily entry asks too much of poor human nature whose engine knocks so badly ever since original sin. What is suggested here is to have a kind of "preaching journal" in which you take the time to set down any *unusual* incident in your priestly life which could profitably be used in some sermon.

At the time when an unusual incident happens, we are all atwitter with the excitement of it, but in a couple of weeks the memory has blurred and vanished. Yet it is precisely these personal episodes that can give color and liveliness and immediacy to a man's talks. Small adventures, yes, but your very own; and they engrave the bench mark of sterling truth on your message. It is the Gospel according *to you.*

This may be the place to apologetically offer advice that borders on the insulting. When preaching, never tell an incident as having happened to you if it did not. There is such a thing as poetic license, but preaching has not become that broad-minded yet. And the results are sometimes embarrassing. I am thinking, for instance, of a priest who was conducting a mission in a large parish. He preached Sunday night and had them on the edge of their benches with a wild and woolly adventure that had all but turned his hair white. Monday morning the second missionary arrived to help with the services, and on Monday evening he told the very same tale, only he told it as having happened to him. From then on the credibility gap became the Grand Canyon.

Finally a preacher's toolbox should contain a set of index cards. A man can have the wealth of the Indies, but what does it avail if he cannot immediately lay his hand on the diamond pin or the ruby ring he wants at that moment for that particular occasion? Let us say your particular wealth consists, first, of a few volumes of your own sermons. By volumes I mean loose-leaf books. Half the size of ordinary typing paper is the most convenient. Then you have your filing system and your preaching diary. The reason I strongly recommend the latter is perhaps because I never had one; but if I were to begin again, I certainly should!

Mark each sermon book *A, B, C, D,* etc. Number the pages all the way through. Call your filing collection *X*; and your preaching diary *Y*, and number all its pages, too. The card index will be a series of cards in alphabetical order touching all the topics you have in your filing system. In time it ought to read something like Abortion, Abstinence, Advent, Bible, Blasphemy, Canonization, Church, Confirmation, Death, Drink, and so on.

Suppose we stop at that last one, Drink. Suppose, further, the

Gospel is about the Wedding Feast of Cana, and you feel that a talk on the abuse of liquor would be appropriate. So you flip through your card index to Drink.

If you have been out a few years, and have been dutifully doing your homework, that card might look like this:

DRINK:

B 42

X

Y 65

Decoded it means that if you go to sermon book B (your own second loose-leaf book) you will find there the talk you gave on January 19, 19--. (The preacher who fears being a bore always writes the place and date on every manuscript. The less you repeat your sermons the more invitations you will receive to return.)

X merely reminds you that if you go to your file you will find material under Drink. Possibly you used some of this in the preceding sermon; probably there is more there that you never used.

Y 65 tells you to go to your preaching journal on page 65 for some personal experience (personal, we hope, only in the academic sense) about the abuse of liquor — the deterioration perhaps of a close friend, the bitterness in a family, and so on.

So you have at least the ingredients of a talk.

All this, I fear, is framing the obvious with neon lights, but I prefer to risk being painfully obvious rather than being irritatingly obscure. At least I mean well.

13 ● How Long, O Lord?

Like everything else, sermon styles change. Helmets have become hard hats, doublets are double-knit blazers, and long, formal preachments yield to casual sermonettes. Reverend Joseph Newton summed it up: "Whereas the preaching of former centuries tended to be noble, stately, rich in beauty and power, in myriad keys and tones eloquent for God, the new preaching is more simple and direct: human, dipped and dyed in the color of life, more artless in its eloquence, more intimate in its appeal."

Say, if you will, that his very critique has overtones of what he criticizes, it is still true that the discourse of older days was much graver and much longer. In early America, for instance, the Lord's Day was the Lord's Day, *all day*. Clergymen like Cotton Mather, whose father bore the reassuring name of Increase Mather, saw to that. Incidentally, it is heartening to recognize that, like the rest of us, he was in many ways quite human. For example, when he was passed over for the coveted presidency of Harvard, he retorted by gathering a sympathetic group to found Yale.

Anyway, his breed of preacher sniffed at the notion of a sermon that lasted less than two hours. Should any weary Puritan doze under their long-winded pulpit, a beadle tiptoed gingerly down the aisle and tapped him awake with a long, rebuking rod. After even two hours, one dominie was known to inquire of his anesthetized audience, "Do you perhaps want yet another glass?"

The glass in question was an hourglass, whose sands had run

to the bottom. "Not today," came the unanimous response, "not this day!" On a similar occasion the preacher had only reached his division by the first hour, and was just ticking off his long list of points to be proven, when one of the hearers started for the door. "Where are you going?" bellowed the preacher. "For my nightcap," came the reply. "From your sketch, we'll be here till morning!"

Not that this was an exclusively Puritan practice. In medieval times and even later, when the church was the poor man's theater, the pulpit never faced the clock. One thinks of marathon orators like Savonarola, the Dominican monk who could fill the cathedral to overflowing and hold them for hours. More than that, without benefit of loudspeakers he would address thousands in the great open square. When his round and roaring climaxes boomed out, the Florentines struck their breasts, flung before him their lutes and perfumes and mirrors and sensual pictures for a great bonfire. It is ironic that Savonarola's own body was burned in the same town square in just such a crackling blaze.

Even in our own day, I have heard hour-long sermons. This would usually take place at a "mission," meaning a series of discourses on such grim topics as death and sin and judgment and hell. Because, back then, houses were drab and evenings were dull, with no radio or television and no entertainment but a wind-up Victrola, the missionary hit the parish like a spiritual meteor. He was half matinee idol and half prophet, bursting in from the desert with eyes blazing with zeal, and lips trembling with a message from God.

He could stand in the pulpit, gilded crucifix thrust into his cincture, and thunder for an hour or more, because this was a sacred week and he was a stranger. But, how long should a sermon be today? Well, how long is a piece of string? Or a bridge? Or a driveway? Obviously the occasion will call the play. Five minutes would be insulting for the centenary of a cathedral. Twenty-five minutes would be suicide at the ordinary Sunday Mass. We were taught from Scripture that the Catholic Church was founded on a Rock. We are not very old in the priesthood before we discover that the modern church is founded on a parking lot.

Still, I knew a man who maintained that in general there was no such thing as a long sermon or a short one. He held that there is only an interesting sermon or a dull one. But even this distinction has to be dusted with a sensible sprinkle of salt.

What he meant was probably better voiced by a blunt parishioner who had the hardihood to tell the preacher, "Actually your sermon was not too long. It just seemed that way."

One grave authority insists that the only difference between the short sermon and the long one is that for the long one you should open more windows. Others take the opposite tack and claim that if a sermon is *good* it need not be *long*. And if it isn't good, then God help us, it *shouldn't be long*!

A close friend in the priesthood confided recently that before he climbs into the pulpit, he reminds himself, "Remember you are the Reverend Father Sullivan. Not the Never-end Father Sullivan." Seems it works, too.

In more than one Protestant manual on preaching I have seen allusions to twenty-five minutes as the usual time allotted for the sermon. In the ordinary Catholic Sunday Mass the quota is closer to ten. The explanation advanced for this wide difference is that when Protestantism abandoned the Mass it concentrated on the pulpit and on the choir loft. On the other hand, where the center of the service is the altar (as in every Catholic church), the pulpit and the choir loft demurely melt into the background of secondary roles.

As a result many priests do not preach too well (they feel they do not have to) and most Catholic congregations do not sing too well (they do not have a choral or a hallelujah tradition). Some trace this reluctance to sing out, "to sing to the Lord," back to the days of the Penal Laws in Ireland when services had to be in secret, and because Irish customs strongly influenced the Church in its growing days in America.

The ten-minute talk after the Gospel, and usually "on the Gospel," is not calculated to develop Lacordaires or Bourdaloues. Besides, the man in the Catholic pulpit knows that if he preaches well it does not mean that he will go higher. A Protestant minister who excelled in preaching might expect a summons or "a call" to a more prestigious parish. The Catholic priest knows that, preach well or ill, he is but an ecclesiastical checker on the board of seniority, where big jumps are a rare and envied exception.

None of this dare lessen the priest's obligation to produce the best homilies he can, for high spiritual motives. If he is not moved by such motives, he should not be in the priesthood. And while the homily is, in measure of time, a lesser part of the Mass, it should not be a negligible or a neglected part. True, it has become a casualty of our hectic, frantic, breathless pace in modern life, insofar as it has been shortened from the old days. But, for that very reason, because the quantity has been cut, should not the quality be improved?

But all pulpit appearances are not Gospel homilies, and it is these more formal occasions that tempt the long-winded. Warnings against such endless meanderings come from highly critical sources. There was the housekeeper who was returning to the rectory with the preacher after a marathon sermon. "I suppose," he said tentatively, "I should have put more fire into my sermon." She snorted, "If you ask me, you should have put more of your sermon into the fire."

There is another tale of the same blunt tenor. Though it appeared in print many years ago, I have heard it recounted as a recent experience. This time the ubiquitous housekeeper noticed that the mission preacher was only toying with the food on his dinner plate. He explained that before a "big" sermon, he never took a full meal. After the sermon, he asked her what she thought of his preaching. She answered simply, "You should have et."

Most sermons that seem long are not long because they say

too many things, but because they say the same things over and over. The patron of such preachers is St. Francis Xerox. If a man has not written the talk, he may come around and around, like a revolving door, to what he said three minutes before.

I forget who it was that summed it up with the acid but accurate observation: "It is a hideous gift that some men possess, to be able to say absolutely nothing at great length." As Hamlet says to the players, "I pray you avoid it." Such a sermon, repeating and repeating, is little more than a long oratorical belch.

It was such pulpit performances that made one crusty English pew-holder crawl out of his leather chair at the club long enough to dash off a sour letter to *The Times*. In what amounted to a cultural snarl, he wrote: "The average sermon I have heard was twenty minutes in length and a half inch in depth." What prolongs some sermons past their prime, is embarking on a sudden new idea. In general, resist the temptation to develop such inspirations. Even though that bright thought starts up before you with all the dazzle of a jewel-winged pheasant, do not follow it. Not now. File it away in the back of your head for another talk.

This applies, too, if you give the same talk, as most of us must, at two or more Sunday Masses. Prepare the talk; deliver it; and do not change it at the second Mass. Sad experience knows that to change is not to substitute, but to add. This means that your second version will be much longer and probably less effective than your first. Here, too, save the brilliant flashes of inspiration for some future sky. Write them down and salt them away. They'll keep. The mind has no fresh food or deepfreeze distinctions.

Common courtesy on our part will always recognize that people have obligations outside the church doors and will try to respect these commitments. If I may intrude the personal (and in these circumstances, who is there to stop me?), I used to make this promise from time to time to the people at our eight novena services each Wednesday. "When the chimes from the church tower are sprinkling their silver notes announcing the hour, you will see little me climbing the marble steps to the pulpit. When the same chimes announce the half hour, you will be leaving the church."

They knew they could make an appointment and be able to keep it. Maybe it was Christianity by the clock, but at least they came. An hourglass would have kept them away. Eloquence in a preacher is something to be wished for, but promptness and courtesy are attainable by all.

All of which makes me remember a confrere (and there is not a kindlier or warmer personality around) who arrived late for the daily early-morning convent Mass. Mother Superior met him with a face like a Vermont winter, and snapped, "Father, you're late for Mass!" Father registered all innocence and complete surprise, and said, "Did it start already?"

One of these days it may.

14 ● The Magic of Words

"In the beginning was the Word." So it is set down in the Gospel, and so it happens with good homilies. First, you have to write it. There are, to be sure, some gifted preachers who can abruptly soar aloft and, without benefit of written preparation, put their talent on automatic pilot so as to keep every hearer entranced till they touch down fifteen minutes later in a velvet-smooth conclusion.

There are such, but I have not met many of them. I suspect they may be as rare as pigeon-blood rubies. Ninety-five percent of us, if we want to offer the congregation something worthwhile, have to do some writing first. Before we speak up, we have to write down. Geniuses aside (and you don't have to reserve much room), it is a law of literature that the easier and pleasanter something is to read, the harder it has been to write. Conversely, the harder and duller something is to read, the easier it has been to write. You don't kid around with Nature.

At the moment some priests are beating the drum for "witnessing to Jesus." As I understand it, this means that your own religious feeling should spurt out of your sermon like a fountain. Let them know that you have met Jesus and know Him and love Him! Fine! But there ought to be a good sermon there first, so that you have a base of operations. Warm and genuine emotion is grand, but if people are to listen, the homily has to be attractive, and if they are to be convinced, it has to be logical. Enthusiasm alone is a straw fire.

Since we cannot, as a rule, hope that powerful phrases and

apt illustrations will hover over our heads like tongues of fire in the midst of spontaneous speech, it follows that for most of us good preaching must begin with good writing. Good writing begins with good words, bright words, precise words, lively words.

Certain words we should not touch with an eleven-foot pole. I make reference not to the four-letter ones, but to the fourteen-letter ones, the absurd and unnecessarily long words. There is even a very long word to describe these: "sesquipedalian" (which literally means "a foot and a half in length"). In the old-time minstrel performances, the black-faced end men deliberately declaimed such jawbreakers to portray pretentious pomposity. We can produce the same effect in the pulpit without meaning to, by serving up the triple-jointed polysyllables.

It is to laugh, or at the shame of it, to cry! Suppose you wanted to describe some medieval knights snatching a bite during a lull in the battle. You could say, "Accoutered in the habiliments of conflict, they partook of the available comestibles and imbibed the current beverage."

But the poet puts the same situation this way:
They carved at the meal with gloves of steel,
And drank red wine through helmets barred.
Case rests.

In our proper Boston there is an elite hotel that wears its patrician elegance as prominently as a dowager's dog collar of matched pearls. If you leave by the main revolving door, there is a sign in huge letters: NOT AN ACCREDITED EGRESS DOOR. Perhaps it means, "If you get hurt passing through here, don't sue us!" Or maybe they have so many doors leading to the street that this one (because it revolves) doesn't count. In any case, wouldn't it be simpler to say, NOT AN AUTHORIZED EXIT?

Leave it to Mark Twain to skewer the error of using the almost right word instead of the exactly right one. "The difference," he wrote, "is the difference between lightning and lightning bug."

I knew a pastor once whose preaching vocabulary gave the

impression of wearing striped trousers, silk hat, gold cane and spats. He never merely "knew" something. Rather he "was not unaware that," or he was "cognizant of the fact that," or he "had been apprised of." If he was speaking before a bishop he salaamed with, "May it please Your Excellency." I thought of him this morning when I heard a radio announcer say, "If you are in the market for business real estate, you should beware of the new firm of" — let us say — "Zilch & Zip." My ears stood up at such frankness. Then followed a glowing ad for this new concern. Now it came to me. The announcer had said, "You should *be aware* of," not "You should *beware* of." If the copy had just said very simply, "You should *know about* the firm of," then everything would have been fine.

Perhaps a distinction is in place here between the spoken and the written word. When you write, the words are there fixed to the page for reexamination in case of doubt. But the spoken word has to be absorbed in flight, almost like taking in billboards from a whizzing car. The written word can be subtle, indirect, sophisticated, elegant, polished. Better that the spoken word be brief, simple and immediately clear.

Words are weapons. Don't burden yourself with clumsy ones. If you mean oily, don't say oleaginous. If the crowd was noisy, don't make it worse by calling it vociferous. Have in your heart the fear of God, not trepidation of the Deity. For a slight service give the man a small reward, like a tip — not a minuscule emolument. Should your generosity overwhelm him and he passes out, revive him. Leave "resuscitate" to those public servants who have to write such jargon in their reports, like the police officer who is encouraged to put down: "I observed the vehicle proceeding along Clancy Street." At least they can't elevate Clancy Street to Belvedere Boulevard . . . though wouldn't they like to!

Words can be interesting in their own right. You might be speaking about Lazarus or Mary Magdalen and naturally mention their home at Bethany. To most Catholics, Bethany is only a vaguely familiar word, if it is even that — something out of the Bible. Does it not take on more interest and an added dimension if we break the word apart like a walnut and show the inner meat and even contrast it with similar words? For instance:

Bethlehem means House of Bread. (In a special sense, that midnight cave was the first tabernacle.)

Bethesda means House of Healing. (Scene of the pool where the angel stirred the waters.)

Bethsaida means House of Fishing. (Town on the Sea of Galilee, birthplace of Peter, the fisherman.)

Bethany means House of the Poor Man. (The home our Lord loved to visit.)

Pointing out the origin and meaning of names or even of words may be a trivial device, but in preaching we need every little help we can get. The preacher's beat is not bank robberies or the World Series, so the ordinary sermon can hardly expect to throb with excitement. True, the Gospel is the "Greatest Story Ever Told," but to impress listeners, it has to be constantly told in a new way. We do this by having a stable of attractive words bright as jockey silks.

If it was a crime in the good old days for Mom to use Dad's finely honed Sheffield razor to pare some stubborn corns, it is a similar atrocity to misuse or blunt a clean, sharp word. Take a word like "decimate." It used to mean, and from its derivation should mean, "to kill every tenth man." For example, if a prisoner escaped from a concentration camp, the commandant might announce that if it happened again all the prisoners would be lined up, and every tenth man shot. *Then* you could rightly say that the prisoners were decimated. Today, like a package that has been damaged by careless handling, "decimate" has to come to mean "massacre." It is the poor word itself that has been massacred.

Somehow that revives the story of the two salesmen who were ordering breakfast in a country hotel. One man said, "I'll have orange juice, toast, sausage, scrambled eggs and coffee."

The other man said, "I'll take the same, but eliminate the eggs." The waiter looked puzzled, but he wasn't admitting anything. In a few minutes he was back and said, "Sorry, sir, but our eliminator is broken."

If the diner had said, "Omit the eggs," or "Skip the eggs," all would have been well. On the other hand, if he had said, "Drop the eggs," he might have got more than he wanted. By the way, doesn't that original word "eliminate" mean literally, "Away from my threshold!" When you break open a word the way you would a tangerine, you often encounter unlooked-for knowledge.

Anna Hempstead Branch stroked it off well:

God wove a web of loveliness
Of clouds and stars and birds,
But made not anything at all
So beautiful as words. . . .

Perhaps the difference between a man and a monkey is the monkey wrench, but an even deeper distinction swings between the vocabulary of the one and the grunt of the other. From animals come only litters; from men, literature. True, it has been pointed out (especially by the picture weeklies that now are no more) that one picture is worth a thousand words; but did it ever occur to you that somebody used words and not pictures to make that boast?

Besides, words can make glorious pictures of their own. This is the whole theory behind the use of picturesque speech. Can you not see the scene vividly before you when Keats writes, "And the long carpets rose along the gusty floor"? Even one word can be a Kodachrome print all by itself: words like scarlet, creamy, ashen, coppery, chestnut, straw, saffron, rusty, plum.

Up and down the verbal thermometer there are many more degrees than cold or hot. It can be frosty, tingling, numb, wintry, chattering. Or it can be, at the other end, steaming, blistering, sweltering, sultry.

These are not particularly long words. They are not really

unusual words — merely unused words. That is, people in ordinary conversation may not employ them often, but when they hear them from the pulpit they will understand them. They do not have them at their fingertips, but they do have them at their eardrums.

In the everyday world of casual conversation we *look* at something. To do otherwise would be to tempt people to look curiously at us. But in the world of writing (and for most of us writing has to be the first step toward effective preaching) we dress up that plain word "look" with many different hats. In the Gospel parable let that angry master not "look" but *glare* at his unforgiving servant. Let David not look but, in his lust, *leer* at Bathsheba. Let the astounded mourners not look but *stare* at Lazarus struggling out of his shroud. Let the blind man not look but first *squint* through his falling scales.

Or take a common word like "shine." Do we not get a clearer picture if you say that the rainy street *glistened*, the distant auto headlight *glimmered*, the tiny diamond *gleamed*?

In the area of sound, too, words can throw off tones like harp strings. When Dostoyevsky was giving some hints to a young writer, he said, "Do a piece for me about an organ-grinder and his monkey. And I want to hear those pennies hop and chink." Following that suggestion, will it not be more alive to your hearers if Judas, returning his ill-gotten gains in angry remorse, flings the thirty silver coins spinning and jingling on the temple's marble floor? Or if Joseph's carpenter's saw at Nazareth groans through the stubborn wood, and his plane swishes off curly yellow shavings?

Sound words produce talking pictures. A watering can clanks down on a garage floor; a light switch clicks on; a trolley sways and rattles around a curve; rain peppers a windowpane; a woodpecker drums on the rough bark; a jackhammer clatters on the gray asphalt.

Call them, if you like, vivid verbs. They are part of the art of interesting. They give action to thought. They are the difference

— in style — between a hot dog and a roast. They offer a wardrobe of colorful words so your ideas need not shuffle in monotonous blue jeans. Use them, and smoke will never merely go up; it will billow or roll or drift or spiral or whatever it is precisely doing. Sparks will never just come down. They will shower or spray or whirl or whatever the situation is. The compass needle will not merely move (everything from racehorses to glaciers moves), it will quiver or flicker or even slightly stir. But please don't make it oscillate. Not even if it is a windshield wiper. There are many words (like oscillate) that people can absorb from the context in print, but heard on the wing go over their heads.

Picturesque speech, like most other good things, can be ruined by excess. Literary cosmetics should not be laid on with a trowel. However, most of us fail not by too much but by too little. Rightly used, picturesque words do not produce "fine writing" in the rhetorician's frowning sense of "precious" writing or pretentious writing or bombastic writing. Actually it is precise or exact writing. It is like the fine tuning on a television set. Its purpose is to present not an overtinted picture but a faithful, natural one.

Picturesque speech is the opposite of vague speech. You do not say "tree"; you say "pine" or "oak" or whatever. You do not say that the dog walked behind the man, if you know it was a fat poodle waddling behind a tilting sailor. Never the general (it is indefinite). Always the particular (it pinpoints the picture).

For another example, consider the word "say." Consider it, and consider better substitutes. The infuriated man does not just "say," he *roars*. The cranky man *snaps*. The sulky man *growls*. The sarcastic man *sneers*. And so on through the whole bilious bunch.

At the risk of piling the plate too high, here is one final "for instance" of vivid verbs. In picturesque writing people rarely "walk." The proud man *struts*, the lazy man *shuffles*, the drunken man *staggers*, the arrogant man *swaggers*, the tired man *trudges*, the determined man *strides* — down to the last entry in the Bunion Derby.

What goes for verbs, holds for adjectives, too. Hands can be "dirty" in a half-dozen different ways. They can be *grimy* with coal, *dusty* with ashes, *blotched* with paint, *splattered* with mud. To find the right word may mean breaking open *Roget's Thesaurus* (my tattered copy is literally broken apart); but that is the way a sentence comes alive and a vocabulary is built.

Phrases that in their beginning wore a fresh picturesque complexion like a teen-age cheerleader can become leathery and creased from too much exposure. The housewife who first smeared that sugary white goo on a cake and called it frosting, saw the white glaze of a winter landscape. Today frosting is only a kitchen cliché. We say it without any thought of its meaning. In fact we speak of chocolate frosting and orange frosting and pink frosting. Enough to make Jack Frost shiver.

Speaking of tired clichés, lay your hand on the plays of William Shakespeare and solemnly swear never to say "a riot of color." That riot was quelled long ago. Or "a blanket of snow." That blanket has been gnawed to shreds by the moths of time. Or "the picture of contentment." That picture has long since fallen out of its peeling frame. Or "the height of folly." To say that, is the depth of poverty in expression.

Recently the clue in an English crossword puzzle was "an old revolver." The answer turned out to be "earth," which, once you are broad-minded enough to forget all about firearms, qualifies on both scores. Some combinations of adjectives and nouns are old revolvers, too, in the sense that they are continually turning up, whereas they should always be turned down.

These are the golden jubilarians of prose, adjective and noun that have been wedded to each other for uncounted years. You have never met them? What about rosy cheeks, pearly teeth, ruby lips, wrinkled brow, golden opportunity, long-felt want, distinct pleasure, ruthless attack, psychological moment, young hopeful, dire consequences — alas, the litany is so long! There are phrases, too, inseparably joined like Siamese twins, which bright writing "avoids like the plague." Get it? Phrases like straight as an arrow, clear as crystal, dead as a doornail, flat as a pancake, flash in the pan (who ever saw one?), vale of tears (yes, but why remind us?).

O. Henry once wrote a clever tale called "Calloway's Code." It is the final and definitive putdown of all trite, limping clichés. It is worth reading, not just for the story but for its implicit indictment of the threadbare in language. And, by the way, doesn't "trite" in its origin mean "worn away" or "worn out"?

Incidentally, though at times O. Henry can be distractingly flamboyant and at other times embarrassingly juvenile, he was blessed with a double-decker talent. He had an imagination as gorgeous as a stained-glass window, and at the same time a clarity of expression as pellucid as clear glass. That combination is, in itself, a minor miracle. In the seminary our secular reading was so restricted that I read little except the classics (Scott, Dickens, Thackeray, Stevenson, Macaulay, etc.); but during vacation, when I felt a little wild, I used to read O. Henry. When some critic hailed him as the Maupassant of America, O. Henry angrily responded that he had never written a dirty word or sentence in his life. Today Maupassant would probably be looked upon as literary Ivory Soap.

O. Henry is famous for ending his stories with an unexpected twist whereby the whole plot does a sudden backflip in the last few lines. But don't sell short his crisp sentences and technicolor style. To read him is to learn more than a little. This doesn't mean to throw away your set of Cardinal Newman. It merely suggests that authors like O. Henry can be "English Lit." without tears. He favored the short word over the long one, the vivid over the dull, the fresh over the trite. And the end result is interest, the goal of the short-story writer, but not to be despised by the preacher either.

15 ● The Mold of Sentences

Words make sentences, which make paragraphs, which make sermons. The universal advice from the homiletic coaches on the sidelines is in favor of the short sentence. If a sentence is so structured that it is a succession of balanced units, this, too, would get the *Good Housekeeping* seal of approval, as being really a succession of short sentences. What they all frown on is the lengthy, involved sentence that rumbles along like a seemingly endless freight train. If it were a river, it would be the Nile, coiling down a whole continent.

The drawback to long sentences, with their many phrases like trellises on a vine, is that they require the elocutionary technique and the dramatic skill of a Sir Laurence Olivier to put them across. The other disadvantage is (as noted in another context) that your audience does not have your manuscript for leisurely perusal, but has to absorb the message as the words fly by. So — if you can keep the sentences reasonably short (some of us can't) you win in two departments: your own easier breath control, and your audience's easier comprehension.

Short sentences can produce a kind of oratorical ping-pong between the pulpit and the pews. They create the impression that you are not so much talking at them as thinking out loud with them. I can imagine a passage like this:

"You tell me that the ideals of religion are too lofty. You say you are not a monk living behind the protective walls of a remote monastery. You are a businessman living in the concrete jungle of the commercial world. This I grant. But I ask you: Where does it say that God gave His commandments only to the cloistered? Read the Gospels, and you will find that Christ is almost always in the midst of a crowd. Does the law of God say, 'Thou shalt not steal or bear false witness or commit adultery — unless you are part of a business community'?"

This direct, question-and-answer style will never drape your brow with the laurel wreath of a Nobel Prize in literature, but it will be understood by the average congregation. It brings theology down from the elegant arches of the cathedral to the place mats of the kitchen table. People may not regard you as a profound scholar, but they will know what you are trying to say.

BEST SERMONS ARE A BLEND

In the world of liquor, expert barristers assure me that the finest whiskeys are "straight" but in preaching, the best sermons are a blend. This is achieved by a shrewd combination of the rhetorical and the casual. If a sermon is wholly rhetorical (that is, a studied and formal composition of balanced, simonized sentences), it will walk into the hearers' minds on stiff, unnatural stilts. On the other hand, if the talk is wholly casual, it will be limp as a sagging sail and have no power behind it. To give the sermon proper force, we need the firepower of rhetoric; but to give it warmth we need the easy approach of one-to-one fireside conversation.

After a soaring period, drop down to a disarming colloquial aside. Offhand bits like, "Come to think of it," "For that matter," "You can be sure that," "As a matter of fact," "Speaking for myself," "To be sure," "At any rate" — all the chitchatty phrases we sprinkle like pepper on our ordinary conversation. Even a sentence left unfinished and hanging in the air, punctuated only by a helpless shrug, has its place in preaching, and can be more effective than a grammatical grand slam.

The goal is communication, however you establish it. It seems to me that colloquialisms and asides do precisely this. Again, you create the impression that you are not on a pedestal lecturing your audience; but you are in their midst, speaking person to person, heart to heart, and there is no cold wall of formality between you.

As to specific suggestions about sentence structure, the learned dons waggle a warning finger against being negative. They scowl at, "He was not industrious." They prefer, "He was lazy." So with "not neat" for *sloppy*, "not brave" for *cowardly*, and so on. Similarly, we make the stylists wince when we say, "They did not consent," if they *refused*; or "they would not submit" when they plainly *rebelled*. It all seems very minor and quite obvious, but the "experts" stress it, so I pass it on.

In another area, what holds for words holds for sentences even more — that is, try to be terse rather than tedious, brief rather than boring in the phrasing:

Why say, "In spite of the fact that he was blind," when you can say so simply, "Though he was blind . . ."

One way to make the sentences compact is to boycott (as far as possible) that word "which." It isn't so bad in writing, but in speaking it can be as awkward as new teeth.

Don't say, "Capernaum, which was a town dear to Jesus." Say rather, "Capernaum, a town dear to Jesus." Don't say, "Gettysburg, which was the bloodiest battle of the War." Say, instead, "Gettysburg, the bloodiest battle of the War." (History buffs, this is only an example. Maybe the Wilderness was worse.) The main thing is, leave the "whiches" to Salem.

Strong writing prefers the active to the passive. Avoid, "The tax gatherers were not respected by the Jews"; use, "The Jews despised tax gatherers." (No negative; no passive.) Better writing often follows a simple statement with a vivid clarification, like, "On the Jewish totem pole the tax gatherer was low man."

The words "is" and "are" will never have a picket line marching around them. Nobody goes on strike against the indispensable. But sometimes brisker words can replace them and pump more energy into the sentence. It is perfectly grammatical and orthodox to say, "Christ was on the cross for three

104

hours." But (and this perhaps comes back to words) doesn't the sentence have a stronger current going through it if you say, "Christ hung on the cross for three hours"? Or how about these: He "was fastened to the cross," or "sagged from the cross," or "was spread out on the cross"?

Better than, "Saul's hand *was* on his weapon," is, "Saul's hand *gripped* his sword hilt."

Conversational English usually puts the language through the meat grinder. It comes out in bits and pieces and blobs and globs. And that is the way it should be. Preserve us from the precise pedant whose ears should be bookends! But the pulpit calls for more unity and cohesion in our speech.

In conversation we might say, "The reason he disliked preaching was that it took so much preparation." But from the pulpit, "He disliked the preparation that a good sermon required."

Not, "It wasn't long before Judas was sorry about what he had done," but, "Judas soon regretted his crime." Even there, "regretted" is weak. Lamented? Deplored? Felt the tearing claws of remorse?

The foregoing suggestions about avoiding awkward sentence structures are so obvious as to be almost insulting. None of the faulty patterns is in itself an oratorical mortal sin, but a multitude of these venial sins (the theology of rhetoric is different from that of morality) in a single sermon can amount to a grave transgression. The composite result piles up a huge hill of dead, disordered slag.

TO SPLIT OR NOT TO SPLIT

About grammatical lapses we should make a distinction. Obvious howlers are bound to make the educated in the audience cringe. A sentence like, "They will scoff at you and they will scoff at I," induces literary nausea. On the other hand only a prissy pedant will wince at a grammatical peccadillo like splitting an infinitive, or dangling an errant participle, or ending a sentence with a preposition. The trouble with your average precisionist is that he cannot compose an interesting sentence, so he concentrates on the gray-paged rule book. He cannot catch the forward pass so he devotes himself to seeing that the white sideline is exactly four inches wide, or whatever it should be. Remember Browning's Greek grammarian, who consecrated his whole lifetime to the enclitic *de*, the latter being about as important, and exerting as much impact on the world, as the sickening "you know's" in the average Yahoo's conversation?

Another device that achieves variety and, as a fringe benefit, emphasis, is inversion. If you stand a sentence on its head, it *should* attract attention, just like a human. And that is what inversion does:

"A mistake he could pardon; a lie, never."

"Here was I born, here I raised my family, here I hope to be buried."

"Dark behind the river rose the silent forest."

Or, Christmas is over. Down come the prefabricated cribs, and back to dark sacristy closets and dusty attics go the chipped statues. Down comes the electric star; gathered up, the synthetic, fireproof straw. Back into carefully labeled boxes go all the odds and ends of a do-it-yourself Bethlehem scene. Gone are all the signs and symbols. Nothing is left — but the reality, the knowledge Christ has come!

Inversion also produces variety, and variety is to a preacher what his row of different-colored paint tubes is to an artist. Or perhaps it might be better to say that variety in sentences is to a preacher what "mixing 'em up" is to a pitcher. First he may smoke over a fast one. Then, the same apparent motion, but — float up a waltzing change of pace. Drill the next one to the outside corner. And so on.

The pitcher employs variety to keep the batter off balance. The preacher needs variety to keep the hearer alert. The pitcher does not want the batter to "dig in." The preacher does not want the hearer glazed and drowsy from monotony. So, after a few long sentences, he throws in a short one. After several down-cadence assertions, he will shift gears to a question. After a rhythmic, balanced sentence, he injects a casual aside. A great deal of it is instinct. But instinct is nourished by observing other good preachers and by imitating their skills.

BALANCED SENTENCES

Speaking of balanced sentences, it may help to recall a few examples, because the balanced sentence can be the M-16 of the pulpit soldier. Shakespeare loved the lilting swing of balanced cadences. Witness the speech of Brutus:

"As Caesar loved me, I weep for him; as he was fortunate, I rejoice at it; as he was valiant, I honour him; but, as he was ambitious, I slew him. There is tears for his love; joy for his fortune; honour for his valour; and death for his ambition."

Or (to parachute from heights to the depths) a few prosaic, made-up samples:

I found the classroom empty, the windows shut, the blackboard blank, the desks filmed with dust, and the big moonfaced clock stopped.

Or:

If Mary was so close to Him at the crib in Bethlehem, so close in the cottage of Nazareth, and so close at the cross of Calvary, is she not also close to the throne in heaven?

Or:

After St. Louis they named a great city; after St. Lawrence they named a mighty river; after St. Bernard, a magnificent animal; and after St. Joseph, an aspirin.

Balanced sentences are rich stuff, and too much of a good thing can induce a kind of oratorical overstuffed feeling in the hearer. Or if you have paragraph after paragraph of balanced sentences, you may create the illusion of a company of hobby-horse cavalry all rocking in unison together. But they get no-where. We are not out to create an effect but to change lives.

Linked arm in arm with balance often walks the device of

repetition, echoing not only the mold of the phrases but also emphasis on the key word:

"I am tired of television, tired of its teary soap operas, tired of its infantile comedies, tired of its insulting commercials, tired of its smug and syrupy announcers, tired of the sex and the violence and the sickening reruns, tired of everything. I've had it."

Climax is repetition that climbs steadily up, like a staircase:

We have suggested, and our suggestions have been ignored. We have pleaded, and our pleadings have been met with sneers. We have formally petitioned, and our petitions have been filed in the wastebasket. We are finished with suggestions, finished with pleadings, finished with petitions. Now we act!

Or:

Lord, send us priests! Priests with the flaming zeal of the sanctuary lamp. Priests with the white purity of the altar cloth. Priests with the silvery eloquence of the steeple bell. Priests with the patience of the pillars that bear great burdens silently. Priests with quiet influence of the holy-water font that sends each on his way with a blessing. Priests with the impartiality of the pews that receive rich and poor with no distinction. Priests whose lives will be like the altar candles, burning out in God's service, and whose death like the flower petals that droop and fall on the very altar. Dear Lord, hear your Church, send us priests!

Some writers hold that the progressive form of the verb, the "ing" gives more "zing" to a sentence. They prefer, for example:

"The soldiers came *tramping* down the gangplank."

"Walls of green water came *crashing* over the prow."

(Instead of *tramped* or *crashed*.)

Who knows? Who can feel a sentence's muscles? We alluded before to the fact that the shepherd's crook of the question mark, planted here and there in a paragraph, sprinkles variety over the page. But questions can also provide power. For instance:

What did these twelve fisherman have? A formal education?

Hardly. Prestige in the community? As Galileans they were mimicked and scorned. Money? They had to patch and mend frayed nets. Influence? The next Roman spear would prod them on their way with a muttered, "Keep moving!"

QUESTIONS, PUNS AND ALLITERATIONS

It is said that the Irish (and I happen to be sprung from transplanted shamrocks) are the great ones for questions. They claim that this started back in the days of persecution when the very children were taught to say nothing to the Crown's men, but instead naïvely repeat the question. Roosevelt once taxed Jimmy Walker, when he was mayor of New York, about this Hibernian hang-up. "Jimmy, why is it that you Irish always answer a question with a question?" Jimmy's blue eyes were incredulous innocence. "Do we, now?" he asked.

Still I mind a time in Kenmare when I asked, "Where is the post office?" And with the gentlest courtesy in the world the answer came, "Is it a stamp you would be wanting?"

At any rate the oratorical question knows no racial boundaries. Cicero was partial to it, and he surely knew his way around the rhetorical forum.

If the pun is the lowest form of humor, alliteration is possibly the cheapest device of literature. And yet I think a distinction can be made. Again there rises the difference between the written and the spoken word. On the printed page the alliteration stands out much more apparent, and is likely to look forced and florid. But the same words, spoken crisply and trippingly on the tongue, can produce a powerful rhythmic impact. You are aware only of the effect, without being conscious of the cause.

Still, of all literary contrivances, alliteration is certainly the most open to abuse. At its wildest it drops to the bizarre level of a circus poster. On the other hand we have to consider the twinkling riposte of Chesterton who deadpanned, "I am not always able to avoid alliteration."

The last sentence of a paragraph will pack an extra punch if it capsules an epigram. Against all the laws of physics, a good *bottom* line can *top* a paragraph like a cherry on a sundae. The idea is to sum up what you have said in a way they will remember. Here are a few champagne corks that pop smartly:

"Such is the history of society. It begins with the poet and ends with the policeman." (Sounds like GKC, but I am not sure.)

Somebody else slipped another picture into the same frame:

"Such is high-school football. It begins with hope and ends in a hospital."

"Half the world cannot creak about in oxcarts while the other half purrs along in Cadillacs."

As you can see, most epigrams are exaggerations. But, then, no one is perfect.

16 ● Picture Writing

When a college professor looks through those shining glasses at his class, he sees a roomful of students who are on the same general educational plateau. Obviously some are brighter than others, but all at least have reached a certain standard of academic achievement. Before you can enroll in "Phil. II," you must have gone through the infiltration course of "Phil. I."

With a preacher, looking out on his Sunday congregation, it is utterly different. He sees before him a decidedly mixed grill. Out there are 150-watt bulbs and also 40-watt bulbs. I don't mean to make it so dramatic as to infer that a Supreme Court Justice will be sitting next to a street cleaner, or a banker next to a barber, or a nightclub singer next to a nun. But it is the prosaic truth that you will have in the pews many varieties of intelligence and education, all the way from grammar-school dropouts to high-domed Ph.D.'s. The problem is, how do you arrange a spiritual menu that will appeal to each, and offer nutrition to all?

No doubt there are other ways, but what I am suggesting here is something called picturesque speech. You speak in images. You avoid the abstract and you employ the concrete. It is as simple and non-shattering as that. Back of it lies the theory that while the uneducated might not easily absorb the abstract, the learned will not be bored by the picturesque. But a vivid Kodachrome style is acceptable to both.

To reduce it to perhaps oversimplification: take two notions like winter and industry, both abstract generalizations. Turn winter into a row of clinking white icicles. Turn industry into a cluster of tall chimneys with twisting banners of gray smoke. To both the learned and the unlearned each idea leaps up, clear and vivid. The less-educated understand and the educated are not bored.

The patent drawback is that such writing takes space on paper, and time in the pulpit. But I hold that it is worth it. Brighter men, I must admit, may disagree. I recall one who quietly but definitely did. Father Frank Connell, C.SS.R. (to my mind one of the modern Fathers of the Church — like Father James Gillis, C.S.P., and Father Robert Gannon, S.J.), occasionally asked me to look over his manuscript before a radio broadcast. If I happened to find in the copy a split infinitive or a dangling participle or an ambiguous phrase, he was delighted. But if I subtly suggested a fresher expression here, or a comparison there, or an illustration anywhere, he would come as close, as his gentlemanly character could, to a gracious frown. He did not argue the point, but he made no change. You went away with the impression that while he knew you had the very best of intentions, you were unconsciously trying to seduce him to waste God's time.

If Father Connell had five pages of typescript, these had to be five full pages of doctrine. No frills. No tassels. No bonbons. And, heaven forbid, no humor! Straight, solid, sober, logical doctrine.

He was sure he had an eager audience. He never said so, but he acted as if the people out there in the ranch houses and in the tenements were tilting their heads toward that radio speaker with all the glowing expectation of heirs listening to the reading of rich Aunt Citronella's will. Or like horseplayers anxious to learn the Derby payoff.

But what realistic preacher can honestly expect such interest? He cannot expect it; he has to deserve it. He has to create it. This may mean that in a five-page typescript, space amounting to a whole page may have to be sacrificed (if that is the word) to picturesque phrases, comparisons, allusions, asides, illustrations, quotations and the like. Call it what you like: garnishing or ornament or bait or tinsel or whatever. The sad truth is that "solid doctrine" is too heavy for the average listener. The castor oil needs its bitterness softened by orange juice.

This is not homiletic heresy. Our Blessed Lord spoke that way. I mean that He preferred the picture to the abstract concept. He did not remind us we had an obligation to give visible good example to our neighbor. He said, "Nobody lights a candle and hides it under a bushel basket."

He was not content to call the Pharisees "hypocrites." He called them "whitewashed sepulchres," meaning a clean, showy front outside, but inside crumbling flesh and crawling worms. Corruption in a Brooks Brothers suit.

He did not say, "It is a terrible thing to scandalize the young (or the weak)." He made it vivid: "It were better that a millstone be tied round such a man's neck and he be drowned in the depths of the sea."

He did not say, "If anyone is rude, do not resent it." He came in with a picture, "If they strike you on one cheek, offer the other."

And ponder the parables. What are they but colored films for the television screen of the imagination? The sower going out to scatter his seed, the prodigal son stumbling back into his father's arms, the lost sheep twisting in the briars, the rich man complacently contemplating his row of barns with the shadow of death falling on his shoulder, the good Samaritan bending over the bloody victim by the roadside — isn't each of these a miniature masterpiece from God's own gallery of the picturesque style?

But at this moment our attention is focused not so much on parables as on phrases. Here the picturesque is achieved by replacing the abstract idea with a material, physical picture. Better, for instance, than the abstruse word "fortitude" or "valor" or even the simpler "bravery" is "the front-line soldier

113

crumpling with a scarlet stain on his khaki chest." Better than "Roman legion" would be "a line of glinting helmets." Just as our Savior knew that better than the "difficulty of salvation" was "the narrow gate."

The Spanish Inquisition will not pound on your postern gate, and the Tridentine Council Fathers will smile ghostly approval if you speak of "the Incarnation of the Second Person of the Most Blessed Trinity"; but Maggy Maguire and Tony Caruso will understand better if you show them God as a pink-faced Baby squirming in a straw-bristling crib, and later a blood-smeared Body spiked to a splintery cross.

Brother Leo once wrote, "Some people are praised for being deep, whereas they should be thrashed for being cloudy." It might, for example, be solemnly impressive to expound, "Among the numerous pitfalls that expose an immortal soul to the peril of eternal perdition, perhaps the most dangerous and most precipitate is that of succumbing to temptations against the angelic virtue."

But would it not be a thousand candlepower clearer and a hundred tons stronger to say, "There are many stairways leading down to hell, but only one toboggan slide: lust"?

In each instance the thought content is the same, but the second version has a brighter wrapper. Notice, you do not change the product, only the package. The machinery that turns out this more attractive package is called imagination. Like hair, some of us have a little, some a lot, and with most of us it thins with age. But, unlike hair, it can respond, at least in some measure, to serious efforts to make it grow.

Usually recommended as an imagination vibrator is the reading of poetry. Personally I find most of the modern stuff misty junk. But the old standbys, from Kipling to Francis Thompson, I dig.

As a diffident postscript in this matter may I submit that the liveliest language and the most pictorial style in the daily paper often flourishes on the sport pages? In the old days of personal journalism, editorials could flame like volcanoes. Now they are often sober, gray-paged treatises.

Nobody doubts (at least I hope nobody does) that in that wide and colorful world of picturesque speech, the one and only king is Shakespeare. You can really reach at random into any play and pluck a vivid example. He did not write, for instance, "We'll rob the monasteries!" But, "We'll shake the bags of money-hoarding abbots!" You can almost see the gold pieces spilling out.

Shakespeare did not dully declare, "Excommunication shall not deter me, if there is any prospect of profit." He wrote, "Bell, book and candle will not drive me back when gold and silver beck me on!"

To him death was not just death: it was yellow bones and powdery dust and grinning skulls and eyeless sockets and a worm like a ring on a skeleton's finger.

He achieves his effect by avoiding the vague philosophical concept and employing the specific physical object. Death is a concept; a skeleton is something you can see and feel and perhaps smell. Shakespeare does not have Hamlet rebuke his mother in terms like, "You married so soon after my father died!" No; he points out that she married before the shoes that had followed his father's body to the grave were old. The interval is measured in something specific and precise and material: a pair of shoes.

When Falstaff reminisces wistfully about how thin he was in younger days, he does not merely say, "I was not always so fat as this." He assures the convivial circle that he was once "as slender as an eagle's talon. . . . God save you, sirs, I could wriggle through an alderman's ring!"

Caesar was stabbed, and most of us would let it go at that. Shakespeare holds up the purple toga and points out the slashes that went stabbing through. Always the picture — if you want a picturesque style.

The trouble is that when Shakespeare writes a scene, we nod and think, "Yes, that's just the way it happens." And we think we are very observant and have the artist's alert eye. As a matter of fact we would never have noticed the sharp details unless Shakespeare had first bumped our head against them. Of so much of life we are only vaguely aware. Like the tinkle of the typewriter bell near the end of the line, there are so many things to which we scarcely advert.

Gilbert Murray showed his own keen perception when he observed that the difference between one man and another is what each can see in the same cubic yard. For that matter, in the same backyard. It is the ideal marriage of observation and imagination that has given birth to most of the masterpieces of literature. Children often amaze with their natural bird's-eye view of things. One remembers the small girl who came home from her first visit to the Museum of Natural History and told her playmates she had just visited a dead zoo.

Some men are by nature sensitive to all that lies around them and react to the smallest things. Nature loaded their brain with highly sensitized film. Other men are seismographs and respond only to something as obvious and violent as an earthquake. Even a polar bear blinks at the colored streamers of the aurora borealis, while a poet can feel delight in the miniature sunset mirrored in a doorknob. Or the cherry glow of a cigar on a midnight porch. Or the black satiny sheen of city streets in the evening rain. And on, and on.

Like any other good thing, picturesque writing can be ruined by extravagant use. Better not do at all than overdo. Perhaps it comes down to the difference between the soft blending of colors in the Mona Lisa and the flamboyant daubs on a circus clown. They are both paint. A little bit of common sense helps in the production of uncommon writing.

We don't have to exaggerate. Lord Macaulay (remember how they used to say, "Everybody reads, everybody admires, and nobody believes Mr. Macaulay"?) — well, the said Lord T. Babington had a tendency to make every minnow a whale. About a certain sultan he once wrote, "Ask him how many men he had murdered? As well ask him how many grains of snuff he had sniffed." It makes great reading. But while it holds your interest, it loses your credence. Of historians in general Augustine Birrell wrote, "Their name is perfidy. If they have a good style, you can't believe them. And if they haven't a good style, you can't read them." Who wants to have his words airily dismissed as "interesting if true"?

Asked to choose between being dull and being double-tongued, the preacher has no choice. But he need not sever diplomatic relations with truth in order to be reasonably bright and moderately lively. One master key that opens the door to interest is the question, "What is it like?" Answer *that*, and you can leave dullness forever behind.

To a large extent literature is founded on the simile. Call it a metaphor, a trope, a comparison, a figure of speech, an illustration — they are all aliases of the same picturesque character.

Somebody remarked of Peter Marshall, the chaplain of Congress, that he said nothing new, but he said it in a new way. In saying it differently a man may reach so far back that it is a cliché, but at least it is a picture, albeit yellowed by time. For example, instead of saying, "This is only the beginning," you might say, "It is only the . . .

. . . *first course* (taken from a menu)."
. . . *overture* (from music)."
. . . *opening gun* (from warfare)."
. . . *round one* (from boxing)."
. . . *kickoff* (from football)."

Or, it could be the entering wedge, the camel's nose, chapter one, the tip of the iceberg, the first large drops of the shower.

Similarly "the end" could be pictorialized:

Yesterday they closed the book on . . .
Yesterday they patted down the last sod on the grave of . . .
Yesterday the last leaf fell from the tree of . . .
Yesterday they drew the sheet over the body of . . .

117

This morning they are rolling up the hoses of . . .

Notice, it is always a material *thing* that is used to express the abstract idea of "conclusion" or "beginning." In similar fashion if you wanted to say, "You would think he was always reading serious literature," it might be better said, "You would think his nose was never out of Emerson." Or, "You would think his thumbprints were on every page of Shakespeare."

But to return to that handle that fits so many rhetorical tools: *What is it like?* Take so common a thing as a tree. What is *it* like? In summer it stands like a great green banner in a parade that has just come to a halt. In autumn it tosses like an Indian warbonnet of gorgeous colors. In winter its bare branches are like black antlers tufted with snow. In spring it rises like a fresh new fountain of swishing green.

In the pulpit, of course, we need not sonnetize nature. We can wax floors or skis but not poetical — not to that extent, anyway. The world of nature is good insofar as it affords good practice. But in pulpit use your "What is it like?" can roam over areas as prosaic as an old shoelace.

Suppose, for example, you are preaching on occasions of sin, and let us say that you want to emphasize that the ordinary temptations encountered in our routine life we can, with God's grace, quite easily master. What may defeat us are the temptations that we "tease" or go out of our way to challenge — the temptations when we almost literally play daredevil.

Here is how we might apply "What is it like?" to such challenged temptations. Suppose workmen were repairing the middle aisle of the church, and had laid a broad plank about a yard wide on the floor, so that people could reach their benches. With a little care anyone could walk down and enter a pew. But suppose they were fixing not the floor but the ceiling. Suppose the plank were way up there. How many could walk that same distance without growing nervous, losing balance, and finally plunging down? But why? It is the same plank up there as on the floor, the very same width. And you are the same person up

118

there as you are down here. Why can you negotiate the one and not the other? The difference is this: you had no business up there!

When we go where we should not go, we are looking for trouble. To one man that plank of temptation may be a tavern door, to another a racetrack window, to another a parked car. What good does it do anyone to pray, "Lead us not into temptation" in the morning, and then pole-vault into temptation that evening?

Get the habit of asking yourself, "What is it like?" Notice in your reading how good writers do it. I have just put down a book where Thoreau refers to Cape Cod as the "bare and bended arm of Massachusetts." When you see the Cape on a map you say to yourself, "That's just the way it is!" But it takes the sharp eye and the technicolor imagination of Thoreau to point it out. And who was it that almost scornfully pointed out the easiness of suicide in the lines:

> The Roman road to the ferry,
> A bullet, a dagger's prod.
> Frail is the lock of the gate,
> You need not wait for God.

I can't recall the exact quotation, but somewhere Christopher Morley refers to the red leaves along the edge of an October forest as "drops of blood among the brush where wounded autumn creeps away to die." And I think Father Tabb makes the same comparison with the Precious Blood, falling like red autumn leaves from the tree of the cross.

Speaking of the cross, what is *it* like? Couldn't we say that looked at from below, it is *like* a huge dark key, the notches turned toward heaven, because it was the cross that opened a closed heaven to fallen man?

Looked at from above, the cross is *like* a great sword plunged into the hilltop, slaying death itself, because it was the death of Christ that won man eternal life.

Looked at from straight on, the cross is *like* a big wooden bookstand, the open book being those outspread arms, the paper

His pale flesh, the ink His crimson blood, and written there for all to read, "Greater love than this no man hath, than that he lay down his life for his friends." Greater love no man had. But God had. He laid down His life even for His enemies; yes, even for the likes of us.

Speaking of "God's enemies" (nobody, in His eyes, is really that, so long as he is alive), consider the poor fellow who is bogged down in a habit of sin. He himself loathes it. He makes routine efforts to leave it. But he cannot seem to crawl away from it. What is *it* like?

You might compare it to a grimy freighter, scarred from knocking about the world, limping in toward port. It runs aground on a sandbank. Out come the tugs. They huff and puff and pull and lug and cannot budge the ship. Then one day comes a tremendous high tide. The water swirls round the hull. Now, when the tugs pull, how easily the tramp steamer glides off the sandbank and into deep water!

It is like that when a sinner makes a mission or a retreat or any spiritual exercises. During those blessed days the tide of God's special grace will foam and boil around his soul, so that with only a little effort on his part he will slide off the sandbank and out into the clear waters of a clean conscience.

So, "What is it like?" does not have to drag in sunsets or fountains or lone pine trees or dimpled lakes. Keep it practical. Keep it moderate. Who has not winced at hearing some florid pulpiteer as he thunders on about how the octopus of this is wrapping its tentacles of that around the something of whatever else? I knew a bishop who spoke that way. We used to call him, "My wild Irish prose."

When you ask yourself, "What is it like?" it does not have to be answered specifically with a "like." Similes and metaphors are best when they are there without that "like" sticking up like a periscope. Edna Ferber writes of a girl "with the face of a Da Vinci cherub and the soul of a man-eating shark." The "like" is buried in the idea, not distractingly neon-lighted.

Or take a phrase like, "The snake rippled down the tree." The image of a tiny stream is built into the verb. Or, "The clergyman thoughtfully tented his hands." Same thing. Too many "likes" will click like castanets and distract rather than illuminate.

But whether we use "like" or "as" or swaddle the comparison in the phrase itself, the main purpose is to be pictorial. Avoid the conceptual; favor the concrete. Someone could have said, "Doubt is negative and unproductive." But what he did say was, "Doubt builds no cathedrals and sings no songs."

It is all a matter of comparison. You compare whatever it is you wish to make clear, with something already familiar to your audience, whether you say "like" or not.

Speaking about a belittler or a downgrader one man wrote, "He would have dismissed the Venus de Milo as a double amputee."

Another man wrote about someone's big hand falling on his shoulder. He didn't say it was a hand large *like* this or that, or as huge as this or that, but: "A hand so large I could have sat in it, grabbed me by the shoulder."

Like or *as* does not matter, but the comparison, the allusion does. It adds clarity and color and life to the text.

Many writers prefer to combine the abstract and the picturesque. They say something first for the intellect, and then say it another way for the imagination. First the idea, then the image. First a preacher might say, "The true Christian remembers benefits and tries to forget injuries." Then he adds, "Carve benefits in marble. Write injuries in the dust."

I have purposely not touched upon "stories" or anecdotes for two reasons. First, they are an obvious device and perhaps are used too often in sermons rather than too little. Secondly, so few of them are clean bullets that split the bull's-eye. Most of them are scatter shot that never quite pierce the target.

The best stories, it seems to me, are those you siphon from your own experience. The incident impressed you (that is why *you* remember it) and for that reason it is likely to impress somebody else. The second-best stories are those dredged out of history or biographies. The latter have name value and this adds to their clout.

Just recently I read something about the painter, Raphael, that might illustrate for a congregation the uncertainty of death. The young never think that the hand of death can fall on their shoulder. But Raphael was only thirty-seven, in the golden prime of his career, when suddenly he was dead. Who would ever have thought that the bony fingers of death would have taken the still-wet brush out of those strong, young fingers, so vibrant with health, so flowing with talent, so eager to reach for fame?

In the procession to the cemetery they carried high on a black-draped cart the very painting that Raphael had been working on when he died, the famous "Transfiguration." Nothing so touched the crowds along the way as that unfinished masterpiece. Here was the uncertainty of life painted as not even Raphael could paint it. And the signature in the corner was GOD.

17 ● Little Sir Echo

The thought occurs that since we just mentioned repetition as a rhetorical excellence, it is only fair to warn against another kind of repetition as an oratorical pitfall. By this I mean returning again and again (like Fido and his buried bone) to a favorite topic.

There is a threadbare tale (though I always liked it) about the father of a family who had the pious custom (and would there were more like him!) of asking God's blessing on the evening meal.

This night he duly looked up and said, "Bless us, O Lord, and these Thy gifts which we are about to receive . . ." and then he looked down and saw on the table a steaming platter of hash. So he looked up again and confided, "Lord, it won't be necessary. All these things *have been blessed* on previous occasions."

How many congregations have to resign themselves to homiletic hash! They are served again and again with an all-too-familiar dish.

So many preachers have favorite themes. To them that particular subject may be the Rock of Gibraltar, but to many in the pews it may be only well-worn gravel.

It is an eyebrow-raising mystery how a magician can, out of the same silk hat, dexterously pluck scarves, pigeons and wineglasses. But some preachers perform this wonder in reverse. Each Sunday, out of a completely different Scripture, they manage to draw out the very same sermon.

Someone was telling me (or did I read it in one of our trade papers?) how Sunday after Sunday the people who happen to attend the junior curate's Mass at a certain church are sure to hear a new, far-out interpretation of the Gospel, calculated at the very least to surprise, if not indeed to shock.

At the senior curate's Mass they will be assured that the only hope for the Church today lies in the Liturgy. (There were, incidentally, a larger percentage of Catholics pouring into our churches for Holy Mass before we ever heard of Missalettes, but let that pass. In all honesty, there are surely other factors.)

At the pastor's Mass, the note will be struck, loud and clear, like a jingling anvil chorus, for the need of money to keep the plant going. Religion may be free, but someone has to buy the bread and wine and candles and vestments and schoolbooks.

If you suspect that you yourself have a favorite topic, in God's name bury it in the sacristy drawer with the soiled altar linens. Can you imagine the boredom and the bitterness of someone sitting out there, Sunday after Sunday, and being served the same menu, listening to the same tune, shown the same painting? One of the horrors of hell is its sameness. Who deserves that now?

Is it cheeky to suggest that we keep a careful record of each Sunday's subject? When I was stationed in a Bronx parish we had a weekly radio program, and the priest in charge insisted that each successive preacher write down in a logbook the topic he had treated that particular week.

Eventually a little transfer card arrived, nudging me to Boston, and there I followed the same prudent procedure, even though here it turned out to be a matter of the same man preaching practically every Wednesday of the year. The curious result is that I could now tell you (as if you wanted to know) what was the topic of my little sermon on the first Wednesday of January 1945 or on the last Wednesday of December 1975. At least the people were not dittoed to death. Certainly there were repetitions, but at judicious and painless intervals.

So, once more to emblazon the obvious: it is automatic that

124

an earnest preacher keep a record of the place and date of every sermon, written at the head or the foot of the manuscript. This may mean that next year you must go out after new material on that particular theme. But it will keep you on your toes. And it will keep them coming.

18 ● The Five W's

In the old, old movies the editor at the city desk, with a green eyeshade hooding his hard eyes, and a cigar stump in his grinding teeth, would bark at the young reporter, "Go out and get that story!" And the "cub" (as he was called, never in a newspaper office, but only in breathless novels) would grab his broad-rimmed hat, snatch up pad and pencil, and hail a cab like Alexander the Great stepping into his chariot.

The starry-eyed young man also took with him, hidden but very real, the five W's, which were the tent pegs of any good reporter's copy: Who, What, When, Where, and (if he could nail it down) the often elusive Why.

Any preacher, attacking a topic for the first time, might well be advised to wheel up the same battery. Cicero and Quintilian called them the *loci communes,* meaning they were like five different taps that you drove into the maple tree of your topic, and out of each some syrup would drop. When you don't know where to begin, bring each of these five W's in turn into the witness box, and you may break the case.

As an example I reach out at random to the most unlikely topic I can think of: a doorknob. Yet, notice how even this, under pressure of three of the five W's, and the other ancient rhetorical aids, produces material that can be worked up into a talk.

WHO?

Who reaches for a doorknob?

I think of a tiny child on tiptoe, reaching up to the doorknob for the very first time and turning it for his entrance into a great new world!

Or a policeman, gripping the doorknob grimly, turning it slowly, reluctantly walking in, to deliver his sad news of a tragic accident.

A star actress, playing a part, her hand on the doorknob, clenching and releasing it in a hesitant leave-taking, and at the same time (as the story goes) winking at the stagehands.

A drunk, his wavering hand groping for the doorknob and slipping from it, as he slides to the ground.

WHAT?

The answer to this can be either a strict definition, or a rhetorical one, or a combination of both.

A doorknob is one of the thousand things we take for granted. One of the important *little* things of life, like a postage stamp or a match or a key or a watch. Size has nothing to do with importance.

As much as anything it is a sign of civilization, like a church spire or an electric chair. It is a little thing that swings open a big door . . . just as a revolution is a minority swinging a majority.

WHERE?

You find doorknobs on doors, but not on tent flaps, not on the swinging doors of a tavern, not on the sliding electric-eye doors at airports, not on the iron-barred doors of prison cells.

CIRCUMSTANCES

Some doorknobs are round. Some square, some glass, some metal, some simple, some ornate.

They are generally smudged with fingerprints, because they are used by everybody — no snobbery or exclusiveness here. They are clammy in foggy weather, dripping in the rain.

The polished doorknob is the clean gleaming symbol of a

neat household. To a poet's discerning eye, the sunset in miniature glows in it.

COMPARISONS OR CONTRASTS

There are other knobs: on radios, on TV's, on safes, on computers.

Consider a world without doorknobs . . . if overnight they all fell off, what kind of world would we wake to?

FAMOUS

The doorknob at 10 Downing Street, or at the White House.

TRIVIA

A hard word to rhyme, unless you say something like:
> *Before you get a store job*
> *You first must turn a doorknob.*

CONCLUSION

A doorknob is something you turn and then walk into love.

So much for the silly exploitation of a doorknob. You, the reader, could probably do much better unfolding the petals of a shoestring or a window pole. I selected a doorknob merely as an example of how the classic five W's and their train could be employed even on the weirdest of subjects.

Don't undersell the five W's. They have done noble service for a thousand years.

19 ● Homilies

Some of us senior priests (the gray around the Temples) are alleged to be so Tridentine in our outlook, so devoted to "the way it was," so devoted to everything old, that we look with suspicion even on a new moon. But you have to admit that in the last decade or so things *have* changed drastically.

Take the Mass. But then it isn't the Mass any more. It is the Liturgy. (Just as it isn't the parish. Now it is the community!) Anyway, consider the changes.

First, we changed the language, from Latin to English.

Then we changed the day, from Sunday only, to include Saturday afternoon and evening.

Then we changed the furniture. The altar, which used to face the tabernacle, was turned around to face the pews.

Then we changed the ritual, from a kind of reverent drone by the celebrant to a ping-pong exchange between sanctuary and benches.

Then we changed the personnel. Up to now the Mass had been practically the private preserve of the priest. Now into the sanctuary slipped the laity, men in tailored suits and ladies in bright dresses, to read the Scriptures and (in some places) to distribute Holy Communion.

Then we changed the music, so that it sometimes happens that a fifty-thousand-dollar organ gathers dust in the choir loft while a fifty-dollar guitar plunks in the sanctuary.

Ironically, the more changes made, the more concessions granted, the more empty spaces appear in the pews.

All this to remind you (coming by way of Australia I grant), of another change. What used to be the sermon is now the homily. This is an old word recently resurrected. The Mass had its sermon; the Liturgy has its homily. According to a slightly sardonic septuagenarian fellow Redemptorist, a homily is a Sunday sermon poorly prepared and badly delivered by a young priest whose assurance far outweighs his ability. If I had at hand the rebuttal, I would give it equal space. Some of my best friends are young priests.

One old usher asked me, "What is this homily business? It sounds like a breakfast food." Not breakfast food, but "coffee-cup chat" comes closer, because in its Greek root the word "homily" means "casual conversation." A nearby dictionary calls it "an informal exposition of Scripture."

In the dawn of homiletics the classic homily probably took the form of a verse-by-verse interpretation of the Scripture as it was read. Later came the development of a sustained topic. Here, instead of pausing after a verse, the preacher went on to read a much longer segment, and out of all the verses plucked a pertinent lesson. For instance, he might have read the passage about the wise and foolish virgins. Then he would put the Scripture down and elaborate on the need of prudence; or on the grim uncertainty of the hour of death; or on the sad probability of becoming like the people one associates with: in other words, birds of a feather will crash together. All the colors were squeezed from the *moral* tubes of the Ten Commandments or the counsels.

During the medieval days of gay doublet and bright hose and feathered caps, the core of the homily was rigid logic, and a pulpit manuscript was like a page torn from a theology textbook.

First came the proposition. Then followed the definitions, with the inevitable scholastic distinctions. Finally the proof, sent whizzing like a feathered arrow, and tipped with arguments from Scripture, tradition and plain old unbaptized reason.

This is not so say that the medieval pulpiteers were utterly devoid of all emotion — just a cactus desert with no blooming rose within a hundred miles. It merely means the *emphasis* was on the logic. But these preachers were well aware that human beings are not only logical, they are also psychological; not just creatures of the head, but also of the heart. Still, they laid the emphasis on intellect rather than on sentiment.

Along these lines such a homily on the necessity of Baptism might evolve like this:

1. *Arguments from Scripture,* citing the verses where Christ commands it.

2. *Arguments from tradition,* indicating how from the apostolic age Baptism was universally insisted on.

3. *Arguments from reason,* showing that since Baptism is the moment of official entrance into the Church, there should be some external solemn ceremony to indicate the passage just as in knighthood we have the touch of the sword blade, or (currently) in citizenship the pledge of allegiance to the flag.

4. *Arguments from the Fathers of the Church,* who consistently taught not only that Baptism was necessary for salvation but that it also left upon the soul an indelible, if invisible, mark. (It occurs to me that a contemporary illustration of this, though not, of course, a proof, might be a blank page of typewriter paper. You hold it in your hand, and you see nothing. But hold it up to the light, and the invisible trademark becomes visible: Hammermill Bond or something similar. We even call it the *watermark.* So Baptism leaves its own real but invisible mark on the soul of the Christian. In the language of theology it is designated by the murky word "character.")

5. *Conclusion.* Here enters the emotional appeal: the plea to treasure that sacred insignia on the soul and not let it be smirched by sordid sin. This is what our Judge will look at when we come to die: not at our diploma, not at our bank account, not at our clippings, but only at our soul

with its sign of Baptism into the Faith. Have we held it in high honor or have we let it become soiled and stained? By Baptism we were buried in Christ. Have we also risen to Him?

To most of us, I think, giving a Sunday homily means "preaching on the Gospel." But here we are tiptoeing through a minefield. The very real danger is that in our talk "on the Gospel," we shall merely *repeat* the Gospel, almost like a prolonged and distorted echo. Having just given out the brief and clear-cut original, now in the homily we proceed to follow it with a faint and smudgy carbon. We say over again loosely, limply, lengthily, shoddily, what the Scripture itself has just proclaimed with taut and lean eloquence. This is unjust even to the unjust steward and a bad deal for the good Samaritan.

But such a talk is not a homily in the strict sense at all. For a true homily you don't just take the Gospel and add the water of words. You take up a magnifying glass and hold it over the text, and reveal what it means in all its fascinating detail.

For example in that Cana Gospel where the miracle centers on water and wine, we can explain the Jewish ritual of washing before meals, and other purifications, reaching down perhaps to the ablution at Mass. Eyebrows will go up if you point out that if the waterpots were of normal size, then each contained about six or seven gallons. Multiply that by the six jugs and you have a red sea of wine for a village party. Here we could indicate that as with the multiplication of the loaves in the wilderness, the generous Jesus provided more than was needed. Point out perhaps, too, that some commentators hold that such wedding celebrations were leisurely week-long affairs. We might emphasize also that the use of the word "woman" was not cold or condescending or disdainful in the original Greek. This is evidenced in pagan authors like Xenophon or Homer. Commentaries have come a long way since last century's MacEvilly (fine as that was); and the present Jerusalem Commentary is (to coin a cliché) a gold mine.

People are naturally curious, and if you can tell them what the widow's mite looked like, or the coin of the tribute, and how much they were worth, it adds local color and immediacy to the scene. Details like these mean a little digging, but the people know and appreciate that you are not merely repeating the Gospel but imparting information.

Such marginal notes can sweep away doubts, too. Remember the man who was tossed out of the banquet hall by the lord of the manor because he did not have on a wedding garment? On the surface it certainly looks like a raw deal. Here is the poor fellow, just brought in from the highway to a "come as you are" party. Did they expect him to saunter in wearing a tuxedo?

Ah, but apparently it was the custom at such affairs (at least so I have read) for a servant to stand in the doorway with an armful of light white capes. You were supposed to take one and drape it over your shoulders as a sign that you joined in the festive spirit of the celebration and saluted your host. To refuse that ceremonial garment was the ultimate insult. Against this background the ejection makes sense.

The advantage of the commentary is that it will help you set the stage for the particular Gospel event, laying out the locale, the time of the year, the coins, the customs, the contemporary flavor. Let us say that next Sunday happens to be the 17th Sunday in Ordinary Time.

Here is a sample (no Treasure of Sierra Madre to be sure) of notes assembled as a practical example. The central theme is the miracle of the loaves and fishes.

INTRODUCTION

This miracle is unique (not just in the broad sense of being unusual or extraordinary, but in the strict sense of being "one of a kind"). It is the *only* miracle mentioned in *all four* Gospels.

It begins with our Lord disembarking. This particular body

of water is called by three names: the Lake of Galilee, the Sea of Tiberias, the Lake of Genesareth. Galilee was the general region, Genesareth the western shore, and Tiberias the principal town.

PLACE

The locale of the miracle was about eight miles from Bethsaida. To get bread the crowd would have had to hike there or to some of the smaller villages in the area.

TIME

April, spring of the year, when grass there was soft and green. People, ranged in rows with bright-colored robes, must have looked like a gay flower garden or like a gorgeous stained-glass window.

PERSONNEL

Philip, who ran his eye over the crowd and made his rapid calculation. He knew that one silver piece would buy twenty-four loaves. So it would take more than two hundred pieces to feed this crowd.

Andrew, scouring the crowd, came up with a boy who had a basket of five loaves and two fishes.

FISH

Fresh fish would have spoiled in the heat. Probably dried fish. Jews used it as a condiment to add some savor to the coarse bread.

Fish were immortalized in the carvings in the catacombs. The Greek word for fish became the code word for Christians. Its letters, *ichthus* or *ichthys,* stood for "Jesus Christ, Son of God, Savior."

In the early age of Church persecutions, a Christian would identify himself as such to another Christian by tracing the form of a fish on the ground with his staff.

BREAD

The bread of the poor was barley bread, not wheat. Usually baked at home — despite the fact there were bakeries and even a "Baker Street" in Jerusalem, although it might take Sherlock Holmes to find it today.

We in the U.S. bake bread in oblongs like shoeboxes. The French and Italians bake theirs in shapes like submarines. The Jews bake bread in *round* loaves with a hole in the center. To carry several loaves at once, a man thrust a stick through this center hole.

Some (not many) believe this was the origin of the phrase, "staff of life." More likely it is just a metaphor for bread as a universal food.

MANNER

A most mystifying miracle. Peter said later, "We had not understood concerning the loaves." Dr. Frank Sheed says it is probably more accurate to call it not a multiplication but a multi-location, because, in reality, not the loaves but their presence was multiplied.

Our Lord did not create new loaves. He divided the original five, and when He divided them, they multiplied. Just call it a miracle. Next question, please.

REACTION

The crowd wanted to make Christ their King. They had just celebrated the feast commemorating their freedom, centuries back, from the yoke of Egypt. At this time their hearts always turned toward the thought of throwing off the yoke of Rome. And here was Someone in their midst who could with a mere gesture feed an army! One loaf would do for a thousand soldiers. They had an instant quartermaster corps!

Christ had been speaking to them for a whole year about His heavenly kingdom, and they still thought in terms of a political revolution!

APPLICATION

Note that our Lord did not set the bread at each man's elbow. The Apostles (and presumably helpers) had to distribute it.

So we get grace from God if we ask; but we have to do something, too — we have to cooperate.

If, for instance, a person has a drinking problem, it is not enough to ask for God's help. He must use that help by obeying his conscience and avoiding persons and places that might tempt him. Grace on God's part, yes; but grit and gumption on our part, too.

The main source of God's help is Holy Communion, and this miracle was a preview of that. Before Christ multiplied the loaves, "He gave thanks, blessed, and broke" — the very words of the Last Supper.

In the typical church we have not a high hill, but a High Altar. Instead of a boy with loaves and fishes, we have an altar boy with bread and wine. Instead of Apostles going along the rows with baskets, we have priests, going along the rail with ciboriums. Instead of Christ being concerned for the bodily needs of the crowd, here is the Body of Christ multiplied for our spiritual food. It is our turn to give thanks.

Now that the notes are there, the next step is to select from them the points you would like to make, establish a smooth transition between them (the picture I get is section after section coming out like tubes from a telescope) and finally hit the application or conclusion hard.

The old-fashioned way to develop a homily (and I do not knock it) is to take a single detail from the Gospel and use that as a launching pad for a talk on some doctrinal truth or some moral virtue. In this particular Gospel an obvious one is this: when the boy offered Christ the basket with the five loaves and the two fishes, our Lord did not give him a pitying smile and wave him away as being more than slightly ridiculous. Christ could have created the loaves and fishes out of nothing, but He chose to use what the boy gave Him.

In that same sense, none of us has much to offer our Savior, but if we lay at His feet what we have, He can use it to do wonders. Once we grasp this, we should never be discouraged. (Then go on to speak against discouragement.)

There is another angle to be considered. Gospel facts, no doubt, can be fascinating, and through them the people can be instructed; but sometimes the exegesis of a passage is miles removed from the congregation's present concerns. For example, some time ago the newspapers were screaming with headlines and bristling with cartoons about a new wheat sale to the Soviet Union. When this happened the previous year, the price of bread soared. When the average "man in the pew" hears the Gospel of the multiplication of the loaves, he is likely to start thinking, "We sure could use another multiplication now! Why is it such a struggle just to survive?"

At a time like this it might be good to try to answer his current doubts. We could use the multiplication of the loaves merely as an introduction and then trapeze lightly to the subject of miracles themselves. We could point out that miracles were necessary in profusion when Christianity began, in order to attract the attention of men and to prove the divinity of Christ. But, as you water a tender young plant and not a redwood, so troops of miracles are not needed now. Some do occur, of course, as at Lourdes. But if God were constantly to suspend natural laws, there would be chaos. God would have to somehow float down the would-be suicide from the forty-fifth floor, and at the same time allow gravity to drop that hamburger on the sizzling grill for lunch. And so on. The point is that you link the Gospel with some subject about which the congregation is at that moment concerned, and over that gangplank lead a Christian point of view into their minds and into their lives.

Scholarship is fine, and every priest should give as much time as he can to the reading of recent works in the field of theology. But the homily is not the place for giving the congregation a postgraduate course in modern speculation. I like very much what Father Willard Jabusch, Ph.D., said in an issue of *The Priest:*

"Christianity is not a series of propositions to be expounded and then intellectually accepted. It is much more a Person to be loved, a way to be followed, a life to be lived. And for most of mankind, it is not the cool reasoning of the philosopher that introduces one to the Carpenter of Galilee, but the enthusiasm of the convert, the fire of the prophet, the images of the poet and mystic, the goodness and hope of the holy man.

"Although both systematic theology and preaching must begin with the same Word of God, the theologian moves quickly toward the universal, the abstraction, the theory. The preacher moves, if he would follow the example of the preaching Jesus, toward the pictorial and the practical. His mode is not that of the philosopher but of the storyteller. . . .

"The sermon time is too precious for a reheating of Rahner or Küng, or for 'Tillich made Popular' or 'Bonhoeffer for the Masses.' "

It is, or ought to be, the fresh presentation of Jesus Christ through me.

20 ● Building the House

So unlikely a source as Norman Mailer, addressing a group of seminarians, once said, "A sermon is a difficult art form. Maybe that's why there are so few good ones!"

While a priest does not approach a homily like an artist determined to achieve a masterpiece for posterity, but like a prophet coming down from the mountaintop with a message from God, he can and should learn the most effective way to communicate that message. If St. Thomas Aquinas could baptize many of the basics of Aristotle, the Catholic preacher can listen to and learn from clever old pagans like Cicero and Quintilian. They left clear blueprints for building a speech, or to put it another way, five simple steps on the staircase to eloquence:

1. *Invention.* The old books on rhetoric call it "invention" (an awkward translation of the original Latin meaning "finding"). The first step is to find (in other men's books or your own thought) your material, your arguments, your examples, your proofs.

2. *Arrangement.* Now you put your material into the proper pigeonholes. Then you list what you have, in a logical, persuasive, climatic sequence.

3. *Style.* Here you take those scribbled notes and turn them into smooth sentences and powerful paragraphs. You take all the different colors of yarn and weave them into a harmonious afghan.

4. *Memory.* Now you take what is on paper and put it into your head. Some preachers memorize word for word;

others require only a sketch. Monastery arches have echoed the loud claims of both groups.

5. *Delivery*. This begins with a careful rereading of the manuscript with an idea to proper interpretation. You may decide to be strong in one paragraph and soft in another, or when you should be impassioned and when to be matter of fact. This is your music score and you are the conductor.

Thus the classic formula. But even from this there are dynamic dissenters. The method just cited calls first for the finding of the material. Another school starts first with the plan. The difference is that each begins with a topic; then one school sees what is available in that area, and from this it sketches out the sermon plan.

The opposition begins with the plan and goes out to get the material, the steel girders and the cement blocks that the plan needs for its fulfillment. One crowd begins with the menu, the other with the larder.

As a rule, I try to follow the latter method; that is, I first look around to see what bricks (or ideas) are at hand and then decide on what kind of house (or talk) they will build. At other times I first sketch out the house (or talk) and then search for the specific materials it needs.

Here are two samples. In the finished sketch you cannot tell which came first, the chicken or the egg; and confidentially it really does not much matter.

First follows the rather full sketch of a homily for Thanksgiving Day. In this instance the plan came first, and was filled in later.

INTRODUCTION

On Thanksgiving Day, the American home is divided into the kitchen and the living room. In the kitchen, women (like goddesses before the steel altar of the stove) prepare the sacrifice of bronzed turkey, with incense of fragrant thyme.

In the living room, men watch TV, while they pontificate on punts and passes, touchdowns and tackles.

So, the home is divided between the turkey in the oven and the pigskin on the gridiron.

FIRST THANKSGIVING DAY

Football, no; turkey, yes. A hunt in the wintry woods. But the feasting came after something else: the visit to the church and the thanksgiving service.

TODAY'S THANKSGIVING

The modern American picks up his turkey at the supermarket. And pays dearly for it. But does it occur to him that he ought to thank God that he *can* pick it up? Without the goodness of God he would not have money to pay for the turkey, or eyes to see it, or feet to fetch it, or arms to carry it, or health to enjoy it.

WHAT WE FORGET

If it were not for the goodness of God we could be groping blind men, babbling insane men, silent men in the empty world of the deaf.

OUR INGRATITUDE

God's gifts thunder down like Niagara Falls. Our thanks hardly rise like a misty spray. If heaven were a mail-order house, it would need a battalion of angels to fill the orders; but the job of handling the acknowledgments could be done by one little cherub with a broken wing. Isn't it true that after an illness we are so glad to get on our feet we do not get down on our knees?

EXAMPLE

Ten lepers were cured. Where are the nine? On this Thanksgiving Day Christ will look down the long aisles of empty American churches and ask, "Where are the ninety million?"

NONE BUT MAN CAN GIVE THANKS

In all creation, man is the only one who can thank. Only he can appreciate the silver lamp of the moon, the flaming banners of a sunset, the gentle waterfall of summer rain, the lace curtain of winter snow, the joy of words and books and friends and love. Only man!

CONCLUSION

Give thanks that you, as a creature, are not a hummingbird but *a human being*. That you are *an American* and not a political slave hauling logs in a Siberian concentration camp. That you are *a Catholic* and that faith has lit its lamps along the street of your soul. It is Thanksgiving, and we have so much reason to give thanks!

In this next homily I tried to think myself empty about all the phases of Mother's Day, arrange them in proper order, and flesh them out with the proper details. It came out something like this:

INTRODUCTION

The average modern home has more conveniences than the palace of a medieval king. Enumerate. But though gadgets and gimmicks can make a model house, it takes more to make a model home. It takes a mother.

Nobody ever learned to say his night prayers kneeling next to a new refrigerator. Nobody ever came home from his first day at school to throw his arms around an electric orange squeezer.

HER ONE DAY

Honoring Mother was in God's law as the Fourth Commandment long before it got into the calendar as the Second Sunday of May. But why such emphasis on this one day? For a whole year of work, worry and wrinkles, Mother gets just one day of cards, carnations and candy. Inside all this is a hidden contract: You, Mother, begin 364 new days tomorrow.

HER USUAL DAY

Never mind *Mother's Day*. Think of Mother's ordinary *Day*. It begins close to dawn, goes on deep into the dark. She helps her husband off to work, and the children off to school. It ends when all are in bed. Is the oldest son or daughter still out? When work ends, her worry does not.

HER WORLD

Mother's Day spent in a mother's world. A world of monotonous martyrdom, pots, pans, dishes. Washing, ironing, folding, putting away. A world of medicine bottles, measles, mumps. A narrow world, bounded by stove, sink, clothesline, supermarket.

HER ROLES

If all the world's a stage, then Mother has many roles — in one costume. Now a queen, her crown a dustcap, her scepter a broom. Now a judge, her court a porch full of quarreling youngsters.

Then (without double billing) she is cook and nurse, laundress and seamstress, maker of beds, scrubber of floors.

HER HOURS

No five o'clock whistle so she can drop her mop and forget everything until tomorrow.

Her average day may run sixteen hours, with sixteen complaints and not one compliment. You could not get a coolie to take her job, yet she would not exchange it with that of an empress.

HER LIFE

She wonders about us before we come, works for us as long as we are with her, worries about us when we are away. She gives her blood to our making, her milk to our nursing, her sweat to our rearing, her tears to our straying.

HER TREASURE

To the rest of the world her little twelve-year-old boy is small change; but to her, he is a headline across the front page. To other people he may be a noise and a nuisance; but to his mother he is the reason the world turns and the sun shines.

EXAMPLE

The story of twelve-year-old Bobby who decided to imitate his father and send out a bill — only he left this on the kitchen table (long, long ago):

What Mother Owes Bobby

For going to the store last week	$ .25
For practicing on the piano	.50
For eating spinach twice...	.30
For just being a good boy	.20
Total of what Mother owes Bobby	$1.25

When he returned from school Bobby saw on the table five quarters. Great! Why hadn't he thought of this before? But under the quarters was the very same piece of paper, only turned over, with the following:

What Bobby Owes Mother

For feeding and clothing him for twelve years	Nothing
For staying up nights when he was sick	Nothing
For giving him toys on Christmas and his birthday	Nothing
For just being a good mother to him....................................	Nothing
Total of what Bobby owes Mother	Nothing

Bobby pushed the quarters into her hand and whispered, "Gee, Mom, I never thought of it like that!"

CONCLUSION

Every Mother's Day we are a year older. Maybe your mother has changed with those years. Not the face or figure of a movie star. Nor the gowns and jewelry of a society leader. Maybe her face is wrinkled, her hands are rough, her shoulders are stooped . . . but still beautiful to God and her dear ones! The rose once pink is now white. She has faults like any human being. If not, she is a walking heresy. But even with her faults, the golden halo of genuine goodness fits her more gracefully than any of the rest of us. She deserves love and gratitude more than just on Mother's Day!

21 ● A One-Track Mind

No matter what your topic may be, there is one rule that fits any theme as naturally as an umbrella handle slips into any hand. It is the oldest law in writing or speaking. And that is unity. What would you think of a hitchhiker who held up a sign reading, "Any place in the USA"? Some preachers are just about as definite in their topics. They ramble while they rumble. They touch all the bases but they never hit the ball. They can make one single sermon sound like a résumé of the old-time "Lenten Course."

The man who brashly tells you that he composes as he goes along, actually decomposes, and eventually crumbles into nothingness. As each new idea hits him, he takes off after it, like a man with a butterfly net. If he is clever, he may come up with a few bright remarks, but even in this he is merely tossing out an occasional bonbon instead of offering the bread and beef of the Word. He is like a man who pushes a tray along a cafeteria counter, and takes a small spoonful from each dish, so that in the end he neither satisfies nor nourishes.

A snake zigzags to its destination; a sermon should streak straight on. At your desk you are the engineer in the cab of the locomotive, with one straight track of topic stretching out before you. Even in a homiletic sense, to go off the track is tragedy. Save any bright ideas that may come for another talk, like an engineer who waves at a station but does not stop there.

Unity makes the stern demand, and to some it may seem unfair, that a man know exactly what he is going to say before he opens his mouth. And it means that once he has said it, he will not say it again. The pulpit should not be a duplicating machine. When you hear a preacher say, "As I said before," perhaps you ought to sympathize with him, because not in his stomach but in his mind something is "repeating" on him. He needs oratorical Tums. The chances are he never carefully thought out the sermon beforehand, and certainly did not write it. We do not type something, and then in the next paragraph say, "As I typed before." That is the supreme advantage of writing and memorizing, provided, of course, both are done well.

This, to be sure, does not mean that you cannot repeat the same *idea* over and over again. That, in fact, is the essence of good teaching: *Repetitio est mater studiorum.* But you do it in different phrases, with different arguments and through different examples. The old black preacher had it right: "First, I tell 'em what I'm gonna tell 'em. Then I tell 'em. Then I tell 'em what I have just done tole 'em."

There you have pedagogy at its peak. But only if you stay away from the same words. "As I said before"? Don't remind them you said it before! Say it again in a new way. Yes; but this isn't easy. Of course it is not easy. Did anyone ever claim that writing a good sermon *is* easy? Is it easy for a lawyer to prepare his charge to the jury, or easy for a doctor to work up a case? Does the priest expect just to stand up in the pulpit and be brilliant? Instant aurora borealis? It goes back to this: the good sermon is the product, not essentially of the pulpit, but of the desk. You read and arrange and agonize and write and *then* you hope for an effective talk. One talk, one topic. Not a diffusive spray, but a single, straight powerful nozzle.

Unity is best achieved by clarity of arrangement. Like the fellow who appeared in the office one day wearing one green sock and one gray, and who, when someone smilingly commented on the combination, replied that strangely enough he had another pair at home just like the pair he had on, we, too, sometimes do not make the most judicious use of the material at hand. Some preachers are Spartan perfectionists for unity; for myself I try to stay on the same sermon street, though I may drop into a few different houses.

Apropos of not much, here is a sketch of a possible talk on the Gospel of the Transfiguration, the only real unity being that all the several strings go back to that event. (This treatment is borrowed from the old method we were given in the novitiate for meditation, whereby you pictorialized the scene, visualized the characters, and personalized the application.)

THE SCENE

Four men climbing a mountain path. The great outdoors. How rarely in Christian art is Christ represented indoors! Perhaps as a Baby in the stable, as a Boy in the Temple, as a Man at the Last Supper. But otherwise He stands on the banks of the Jordan, marches under the hot sun from village to village, sits in the boat on the Sea of Galilee — which He knew in its satin smoothness and in its wild stormy froth.

On one occasion He climbs a mountain to fast, then another mountain to pray, then a third to preach. In the wilderness He is tempted by the devil; in the open spaces far from dwellings He multiplies bread to feed the multitude. So often outdoors — no fly on a library wall was the vigorous, moving Christ.

PERSONAE

Peter and Andrew, James and John. James and John were brothers; so were Peter and Andrew. These were the first four followers of the Savior.

He had chosen these to be with Him when He pushed the mourners back and lifted back to life the pale dead daughter of Jairus. He would take these same three when He endured His agony in the Garden of Olives.

They were all forthright, outspoken men — the extroverts of today. Peter was the impetuous leader who sliced off the servant's ear. James and John had asked Christ to bring down the brimstone of Sodom and Gomorrah on a village that had not welcomed Him warmly. To only these three Apostles our Lord had given nicknames, dubbing Peter "The Rock," and James and John, "Sons of Thunder."

Was the Savior drawn to these three because of their outgoing nature, or did He (as a novice master might see it) know that they needed finer honing than the rest?

The other persons were Moses and Elijah, the Law and the Prophets. Then the glittering glory, the Voice booming like the surf, "This is my beloved Son!" And Moses and Elijah melted back into the mist of the background, and the Apostles *"saw no one but only Jesus."*

LESSON

Life can be complicated. We meet all kinds of people, face all sorts of problems; but the idea is to keep it simple, not to lose sight of our main goal. How blessed the man who lets everything melt into the background and *sees only Jesus,* only the serving of his Lord!

If we had to ascend a mountain (not Tabor but Truth) with three friends, and instead of Moses and Elijah, there were unrolled the Commandments of God and the duties of one's state in life, would a voice say, "This is my beloved son . . . or daughter"?

That is why we go in spirit to another hill, Calvary, where Christ is lifted up not on a cloud but on a cross, where He is not transfigured with glory but transfixed with spikes, where He hangs not between Moses and Elijah but between two thieves, where golden rays do not leap out of Him but spurts of blood. We are grief-stricken, but the words that escape our Lord's parched lips comfort us: "Father, forgive them, for they know not what they do!"

Perhaps we do know, at least in a measure, but out of the fountains of His wounds flows forgiveness so that even our shoddy soul is transfigured into the brightness of His friendship.

149

22 ● Text and Intro

A Victorian preacher would no more dream of beginning a sermon without announcing a text than he would of venturing out on an overcast day without his neatly folded umbrella. The opera had its overture; the sermon, its stately text. Even today there are many preachers who hold that the text is to the talk what the launching pad is to the rocket, or the torpedo tube to the torpedo: not something just traditional or ornamental, but necessary and essential. It is the Scripture text, they will say, with its special, built-in spiritual power that sends the sermon into action.

Lately though, at least among many Catholic clergy, the text has ceased to be so sacrosanct. Like the winding carriage drive leading up to the stately pillared mansion, the introductory text is becoming rarer and rarer. So are the mansions; so are formal sermons. On an august occasion some priests will preface their discourse with an impressive text. For an ordinary homily they will plunge right into the pool.

In that post-Tridentine period when we were young (where are all the maniples gone?) there was a lifesaving little black book confidently called *The Divine Armory of Holy Scripture*, and we relied on it religiously. A superb index covering every topic from "Absolution" to "Zeal" always provided a pertinent, surefire text. Possibly the little volume is no longer in print, but in its day it was the answer to many a preacher's prayer.

Personally (as if that made any difference) I do not recall using a text more than half a dozen times in a harried homiletic life. For this there may be two reasons. One, in delivering an introductory text, there is a thin line between being serious and being pompous. Two, such a formal beginning may promise more than you are prepared to deliver. A stately text is like a footman in uniform opening the door: the audience may expect almost royalty to walk through.

Do not get me wrong. In *the body* of the sermon there is nothing like strong, backup texts to give sonorous authority to your words. Pretty rhetoric is only like colored Scotch tape to hold down a point compared to the clean-driven spike of a verse from the Gospel. It gives the talk, in Madison Avenue language, clout.

In oratorical power the Scripture is confounding. "Is not my Word, says the Lord, like a hammer shattering rocks?" In beauty it diffuses around a human message the golden aura of the supernatural. It leaves mere logic behind and steps into the Promised Land of the guarantee of God. You are presenting, as it were, a letter of recommendation from the Almighty.

Some preachers too enthusiastically twist a text like a pretzel to fit over the situation they have at hand. There comes to mind a verse from the old Latin breviary, and I quote only from memory: *"In meditatione mea, exardescit ignis"* ("In my meditation a fire flares up"). How many times in the novitiate and the seminary we were exhorted on that premise to be fervent in our mental prayer! Such an "applied sense" would have some exegetes popping aspirins.

Incidentally, the word "text" comes from the Latin past participle, *textum*, meaning "woven." Our commercial word, "textile," is from the same root. Perhaps the idea is that the opening text gives you a snippet or a swatch from the fabric that is to follow.

In contrast to the homily which springs from a text, some preachers prefer the *topical* approach, meaning that the sermon door swings open on the hinges of a current newspaper item, or an arresting quote from a book just read, or a recent en-

151

counter with an interesting personality, or the like. This has the double advantage of being contemporary and personal.

The aim of an introduction is to establish good relations with your audience and arouse interest in your subject. Should you, then, begin the sermon with a dramatic drumbeat, that is, some rousing, provocative intro? Most experienced speakers (if you can be guided by the literature) shake forbidding heads, purse primly disapproving lips, and waggle long no-no fingers. They argue that while this may be ideal bait for the written word, where you have to set the hook at the first touch, it is too abrupt for the average listener who has not yet settled down, and will still be there in any case for the second sentence or even the second paragraph.

There have been, of course, glorious and oft-told exceptions, as when Father Tom Burke, the famous Dominican, mounted the pulpit, flashed his angry blue eyes on the congregation, and roared, "To hell with the Jesuits!"

While the congregation gasped, he followed his blockbuster with (to really mix a metaphor) a diluting chaser: "That is what the enemies of the Church are saying today." And then, of course, came the incisive, withering rebuttal.

In the same vein Henry Ward Beecher once looked down upon a sweltering congregation in a Southern meetinghouse and solemnly began, "It's a G-- D--- hot day!" Only he did not fire blanks. But then he went on to denounce blasphemy and to condemn the flippant and trivial use of the name of the Almighty.

Such sudden salvos are certainly not to be recommended, because, for one thing, very few preachers can successfully carry them off. One smilingly remembers the moldy yarn about the young American priest traveling in Italy who heard a huge Florentine monk begin his mission sermon by thundering, *"Inferno! Inferno! Inferno!"* Between each word came a pointed pause, and at each pause the glorious voice seemed to drop an octave, and the very word seemed to crackle with vivid fire.

When the young American priest returned to Hackensack or

Hoboken, he decided to try it. So, he began his next sermon, "Hell! Hell! Hell!" But with his light voice it came out like the shrill squeak of an anemic canary. The congregation tried not to smile.

Everybody agrees that a good introduction should lead easily and naturally into the subject; if it does not, the audience will feel that no matter how fascinating the beginning, they have been swindled. An elegant foyer, but the wrong house.

Someone has said that (if it can be done) a foolproof introduction is an interesting definition of your key words. One recalls the preacher who was presenting an appeal for missionaries to the heathen. He began by pointing out that the word "missionary" and the word "Apostle" were the very same. "Missionary" was the Latin word, and "Apostle" the Greek one; but literally they both meant exactly the same: one who was sent. In the same way, he pointed out, "heathen" was an old Anglo-Saxon word used to describe the people who lived in the heath or the heather, that is the sparse, desolate places far from the town. That last idea was new to me, and my attention was snared.

In somewhat the same vein, that is, playing on the key words of the theme, a talk on the recently canonized St. Oliver Plunket might begin like this:

We have all heard of Oliver Twist. Many of us know something about Oliver Wendell Holmes, both the poet and the jurist. If we are Irish, we possibly know too much about Oliver Cromwell. But we probably could pour into a thimble all we know about Ireland's rebuttal to Oliver Cromwell, another Oliver who took the curse off the name: the martyred archbishop of Armagh, the successor of St. Patrick, St. Oliver Plunket. At least till lately that is the way it was with me, and in that light I presume to tell you his fascinating story. . . .

Obvious? Perhaps. But only if many of your hearers would have gotten the same idea. Curiously, they seldom do. The obvious is often overlooked until it is pointed out. Then there is immediate recognition. An idea is somewhat like a lost golf ball: it was there all the time, and when you discover it, you wonder how you missed it. In these areas the Shakespeares have the sharp eyes.

Some preachers like to begin with a catchy quote (if they can get one) like: "The second most deadly weapon in the world is the hydrogen bomb. The first is the human tongue."

Not a bad introduction for a sermon on scandal. The disadvantage is that unless what follows is just as picturesque, the listener may feel a mild letdown. Of the whole sermon suit, he may remember only that first startling purple patch.

Another ear-catching device is an intriguing question. One preacher began by asking, "What, do you think, is the most beautiful word in the English language?" He proposed a few sweet sounders like "melody" and "vermilion" and "murmuring" and "lagoon," and told how one poll had selected "cellar door." But then he went on to play his trump, and say that the most beautiful phrase of all is, "Thank you!" Or it could be, "I'm sorry." Or, "I love you" — depending on his conviction or his theme.

An episode from history, a smiling bit of trivia, a custom from long ago — any of these swings open a handsome gate to the topic. You might begin:

"Everybody, or almost everybody, knocks on wood. Do you know why?" And then paint the background of the medieval peasant pausing to pray at a wayside cross before he goes on as farmer or woodchopper to his work in the woods or the fields. After his brief, rough prayer at the wayside shrine, his calloused hand would reach up and reverently touch the cross. If later that day the sky grew black and thunder roared, or if a wild animal growled in the forest, again his hand would reach out and he would say his prayer. Only now, since he was far from the wood of the wayside cross, he touched the nearest wood, maybe the wooden shaft of his plow or his hickory ax handle. To him it was not superstition. The wood was a substitute for the cross.

Such an allusion would be a natural introduction to a talk on superstition. Or the "knocking on wood" could be the banner leading the parade of the bad use of good things, like taking the Holy Name in anger, or consuming too much alcohol, or the like.

Another opening gambit is the *forthright question*, with challenge in its spine, that makes the audience sit up and look at you with alert, attentive eyes. If you were preaching on the melancholy truth that more people are leaving the church today and fewer converts entering, you could, to be sure, begin by the sober statement, "Recent statistics reveal that there is a marked erosion in church attendance and a notable decline in the number of converts." But you would get crisper attention if you flung out the question, "Why are there today so many dropouts from religion? Why are there so many deserters from the army of Christ? Why is the rate of defection so high and the percentage of recruits so low?" *Then*, throw in the original statement about the statistics. A question intrigues; a statement clarifies.

When you have ticked off all the usual devices to achieve instant interest (and they dangle like keys on a ring) probably the master key is the introductory story. Not any story, but a story that is both appropriate and absorbing. There are dull stories that should never be told; old stories that have the rings of countless years on their ancient redwood trunks; pointless stories that do not illuminate the present subject at all. The best stories come from either one's own personal experience or from biography or history. The more obscure the source, the less chance of its being a dreary repetition.

Tastes vary, and one man's mushroom is another man's stomach pump; so it is with diffidence that I cite a sample story that recently appealed to me. It is no anecdotal curtain raiser with a clever O. Henryesque twist; but on the other hand it is not an excavated fossil like St. Patrick and his shamrock, or St. Pius X and his mother's wedding ring. I cannot recall where I read or heard it, and so cannot give due credit.

Briefly, Rupert Brooke, the English soldier-poet who died in World War I (he was the counterpart of our Joyce Kilmer), one day shouldered his way through the throngs at a Southampton pier to board ship for the United States. Suddenly it struck him that all these people were there to see off relatives and friends. But no one was seeing him off; and all at once he felt a huge, aching loneliness. Then he noticed a boy, about ten or twelve, bouncing a ball at the side, obviously just there for the excitement of departure. So he slipped the lad a few shillings and said, "Look, son, when the ship moves out, all I ask you to do is to wave to me. I'll be in the stern of the ship and I'll wave this white scarf. You just keep waving as if you were seeing me off."

And the preacher went on to point out that life itself can be a very lonely voyage, even though there are people all around us. In the middle of a crowd you can be desperately alone. And the human heart craves company, craves comfort, craves courage. Sometimes the only one who knows us is God. But we don't have to bribe Him to wave to us. All we have to do is tell Him we love Him. He will take it from there.

This opening device of a story, an incident, an episode, is as common in preaching as a handle on a door — and as useful. You gain points if the story is a personal experience. You lose points if the tale is twice told, or thrice told, an archaeological chestnut, ancient and honorable, no doubt, but as tedious as a summer television rerun.

On the other hand (or lip), if the opening story is too gripping and dramatic, you have already shot your bolt, so what do you shoot next? Having led your ace, what do you play now? If you start with the best wine, and then weaken off to a poorer vintage, the audience may feel somewhat cheated and a bit resentful. As the king of Siam once sagely observed, "It is a puzzlement."

When the introduction can be plucked right off the occasion, like a rose off a bush, you have it made, and this is usually true when there is an "occasion." One thinks of Massillon in the pulpit of Notre Dame with the corpse of Louis le Grand lying in the black-draped center aisle: "We come to bury Louis the Great. This casket should remind us that only God is great."

On a more prosaic level I recall how once the Gospel of "No man can serve two masters" came during the football season. It seemed a natural tie-in to begin that homily with the souvenir vendor who had been standing outside the stadium the preceding Saturday. The whole right side of his shabby gray overcoat was completely covered with tiny gilt footballs sporting the ribbons of Boston College. The left side had the same little footballs with the colors of Holy Cross. Similarly his left hand thrust out pennants with B.C.'s maroon and gold, and his right the purple of the Cross. And as the crowd swirled past him, like water around an island, he was shouting, "B.C.! Holy Cross! Holy Cross! B.C.!"

He was the perfect symbol of absolute neutrality. Why not? He was serving the Almighty Dollar and he had to be neutral. But when you serve Almighty God you never can be neutral. You have to take your stand. In the moral world, the spiritual world, no man can serve two masters.

In an introduction it never hurts to underplay one's own importance with a touch of pale, clerical humor. For example, if you were announcing to the parish some special celebration like a jubilee or a First Mass or even a novena, you might begin: "Not even my mother thought I looked like an angel, but this morning I do feel like one of the angels of Christmas, because I bring you good tidings of great joy, which I hope will be for all the parish. . . ."

Or if you happen to be short and thin, as I am, you might say, "You may be vaguely wondering who is the little stranger in the pulpit. And isn't he little! I suppose that if I were to stand at the Communion rail in this black Redemptorist habit, from the back of the church I would look like a little thin black telephone wire. And that is about all I am. Only I hope that the voice of God is at the other end of the wire, and that you at this end listen to the message. It is that in your charming church we begin today. . . ."

There is all the difference in the world between this quiet, self-mocking approach and a groveling apology. You may of course be convinced that the occasion is of towering importance and that your own oratorical talents could be poured into an eyedropper. Nevertheless, all the books sternly counsel against apologies. Benjamin Disraeli, who built his oratorical ability on work and failure and struggle and ultimate success, knew this feeling of possible disaster more than most, yet he laid it uncompromisingly on the line: "Never apologize! Your friends do not need the explanation and your enemies will not believe it." Think positively. Speak confidently. Why should the messenger of God be timid?

Another gambit, in an extraordinarily striking church, might be to praise it for its spectacular beauty. But then go on to point out that the glory of a church is not its marble sanctuary, not its graceful arches, not its gorgeous stained-glass windows, but its people. "No church can ever have a more beautiful ornament (not stately statues, not glowing paintings, not massive pillars) than parishioners in its pews. All the other adornments are put there; but *people come*, because they believe and they love. Now this evening in your elegant church we begin a triduum in honor of. . . ."

The old oratory textbooks used to call it *ad captandam benevolentiam* ("to gain goodwill"). People have not changed. They love to be recognized. Things have changed (from jitneys to jets); but old human nature, like ole man river, just keeps rollin' along. The effective preacher knows his flock as well as his faith.

The indirect approach to a topic can also be intriguing in its own oblique way. Suppose you were talking about the First Communion Mass of the previous Sunday. The congregation would not know what you were leading up to, if you began:

"The Associated Press did not cover the story. All the local radio stations ignored it. Neither NBC nor CBS sent a camera crew. There were no extra planes or trains coming into the city. There was not even an extra traffic detail. If you did not know otherwise, you might think nothing extraordinary was happening

158

at all. But it certainly was. Here in this church thirty-four children were receiving for the very first time the body of Jesus Christ. Thirty-four little hearts who were more worthy to hold Him than the most precious and elegant chalice on any cathedral altar.''

And so on. You might go on to wonder: When will they receive for the *last* time? How often will they receive in between? Will there be a Judas among them, as there was at the Last Supper, at that First Communion the world ever saw? Will there be perhaps a saint? Does it take you back to the memory of *your* First Communion?

One final thought about the introduction, and I grant you it is as evident as red tomatoes in a green salad. Make the intro short. It is not written in the beatitudes, but when it comes to a homily introduction, blessed are the brief! One person complained to the parson, "Why do you take so long to get to the point? You keep us so long on the porch that we never really get into the house!" Another grumbling parishioner told his meandering preacher, "You are endlessly setting the table, while we are hungry to sit down. Get on with it. Bring in the victuals!"

23 ● Divide and Conclude

If a sermon is logical in even the loosest sense of that word, it will have a division, even though that division be no more sophisticated than head, body and tail. Or, introduction, substance and conclusion.

Some old classic French sermons had more divisions than Napoleon's army. On the other hand, Quintilian, who had heard his share of classic harangues in the Forum, complained that a speech without a plan or division was like a ship without a helmsman. It tended to wander in weird circles, going over the same ground, or rather water, and making no progress whatsoever toward port.

One school holds that the divisions of a sermon should not only be sharp but should also be announced, because since a sermon is not to be leisurely read, but heard on the wing, the division helps the listener to follow the line of thought. This is somewhat like announcing the stations on a railway.

The other school maintains that such emphasis is like showing the man the hammer before you hit him on the head. They argue that if you hit him, he will know. They would want the points of the sermon to be like the poles on a grapevine; there, to be sure, but not conspicuous. The purpose of the poles is not to stand out but to support the fruit.

A prime advantage of a division is that it discourages backtracking. Dr. Frank Sheed used to say of a certain archbishop, these several years recumbent in his cathedral crypt, that he would begin a talk by saying something about Christ, and then would say something about himself, and after a while you did not know which of the two he was talking about.

A good division is an arrow and not a boomerang. It always presses forward and never returns to where it was. It covers a point, drops it and takes up the next. It realizes that a sermon should not be a stew with everything mixed together, but a chow line where each new portion is slapped down in its own hollow on the tin plate. And tin plates don't accommodate too many portions.

As to the conclusion, even the most freewheeling experts (an expert is anyone from out of town) agree on this: you should put more work into your conclusion than into any other part of your talk. Prepare the sermon, they say, by reading and pondering and scribbling out just four or five lines of sketch (if that is your way); but write that conclusion out!

Archbishop Sheen went so far as to say that it was his practice to spend more time on the final paragraph of his speech than on the whole rest of it together. Concentration like that evolved perorations like this, "If Truth wins, we win! If Truth loses . . . ah, but Truth cannot lose!" If you think conclusions like that come easily, turn out a few. A blessing which I wish you all. In the name of the Father, and of the Son, and of the Holy Spirit. Amen.

If the conclusion keeps concluding, the congregation squirms with the helpless, frustrated feeling of people in a plane kept in a holding pattern till the runway is cleared for a landing. Long conclusions tend to gurgle out like a leaky faucet or sputter out like a dying vigil light. They end with a whimper instead of a bang.

Of course there is the absurd opposite to this also. "Well, I'm afraid that's all the time we have. In the name of, etc." This abrupt, one-sentence conclusion gives the listener the impression he has just stepped down an elevator shaft. Only one step, but it is a whopper. Still, even that is no worse than the truck-garden sign-off. This is the one that keeps piling up the lettuce.

161

You know, "Let us . . . let us . . . let us. . . ." If during the homily you have given them solid meat, you can skip the lettuce at the end.

Yet, it is admittedly a good deal easier to mock the "let us" finale than to find a satisfactory substitute. What do you say instead? Will it be, "May I suggest. . . ." Or, "Did you ever think of. . . ." Or, "Shall we not in the future. . . ."? There is, to be sure, always the blunt imperative: "Pull that barge, tote that bale!" Or something like, "I know you will light the Advent wreath in your homes and let its light shine on your lives these bleak December days till the brighter light of the Christmas star floods your waiting hearts."

The last line does not have to be an exhortation. Be wary of ending with a sledgehammer series of "You, You, You," especially if it seems to imply that the preacher is looking down from a lofty minaret on the squirming life below.

The ideal conclusion (rare as a day in June) builds up to a brief but forceful crescendo, or fades out smoothly and serenely with some capsule thought they can remember. It may be the only thing they will remember (it is the last thing you say), so it should be the best phrased. If the body of the speech makes its appeal to the mind, the conclusion usually plucks at the heart. This calls for that tightrope walk between emotion and emoting.

In a worldly speech, the conclusion is the place where the speaker lays the check at the customer's elbow. He asks for action: he wants you to buy his mousetrap, or acquit his client, or vote for his candidate. Basically, it is the same with a sermon. The preacher pleads that we start saying that daily rosary, or give up that bad habit, or forgive that neighbor, or do this or that during Lent. He, too, wants action.

The main thing is not to make the conclusion another main body of the speech. Somebody said that an alligator is all tail, but a sermon shouldn't be. An ideal conclusion is the one that brings the preacher to a stop when everyone would like him to keep going. Of theatrical audiences George M. Cohan used to say,

162

"Always leave them laughing." The wise preacher leaves them wanting more.

In your own experience as a listener, when you were in the pews and some prelate was preaching, did you ever hear any more welcome or heartwarming words than, "In conclusion"? That phrase is eloquence at its Alpine summit.

24 ● On Your Mark!

Even before you start your sermon, stop! Not to count the house, but to give the people a brief chance to settle down. *You* may be ready and "rarin' " to go, but they may still be wondering whether they turned off the oven, or how they can arrange a convenient appointment at the hairdresser's. Secondly, a pause will subtly let them know who is in command: you. It will emphasize that you are not nervous (or should not seem to be) and that you stand before them with the authority of the Almighty and a message you will deliver in His name.

Nevertheless, though you enter as an ambassador with credentials from heaven, it is better that your opening words be quite informal and casual, not solemn or dramatic. The chief impression you want to make at this moment is that you love the congregation with the love of Jesus Christ, and that you stand there, in a strange blend of humility and power, to bring them the Good News.

Above all, never begin with any trace of irritation or sourness or sarcasm. If you do this, you would have done better not to have begun at all. You must first make them receptive, if they are to receive your message with profit. This is achieved by graciousness in your manner and an obvious concern for their spiritual well-being. It is something they can sense instinctively, almost before you have said three sentences.

If you feel apprehensive, congratulations! You are normal. Adrenalin is part of oratory. The plow horse just stands and blinks; the thoroughbred prances nervously. There was no more stirring preacher in his day than Phillips Brooks (though most people remember him only as the author of "O Little Town of Bethlehem"), yet he used to tell his friends that he never stood up to speak without feeling nervous.

No matter how long a man has been in the priesthood, no matter how white his hair or rich his experience, he should always carry into the pulpit at least some degree of apprehension. The preacher who is certain that he is going to deliver a good sermon probably has a marked-down price tag on his own standards.

God's hand may be on our shoulder, but if we know our personal shortcomings, we shall climb those pulpit steps very humbly. Herald of the Most High, yes; but one glance into the very slim book of our talents, and another look into the very thick volume of our faults, should convince us that of ourselves "we just ain't much." Weighing the message against the messenger should help us keep that fine balance between His strong authority and our anemic ability.

The very best defense against excessive nervousness is painstaking and thorough preparation. If we have done our part, God will do His.

As a rule the opening sentence of a talk should be unstudied and informal. You cannot walk into people's hearts or into their confidence on stilts. If they sense that you are relaxed, they will be relaxed; and a relaxed audience is a receptive audience. Begin with a warm and friendly manner, and you lay out for yourself the red carpet for easy entrance into their goodwill.

In the days before loudspeakers, the preacher's first concern was to be heard. Often this meant using so much effort that from the outset the man in the pulpit sounded aggressive, in fact almost threatening and angry. Nowadays, thanks to our era of electronics, this is both unnecessary and unwise.

So, don't startle them by coming on like a screaming fire siren. The old couplet for tyro preachers is still a capsule of sage counsel:

Begin slow, speak low,
Gather fire, rise higher.

But don't stay too high for too long. Otherwise your most telling points will sound like the shrill, whistling feedback from a loudspeaker.

Sometimes, as at a Sunday Mass, you can take advantage of the person who has just read the Scripture before you. Go for contrast. If you follow a droner, begin lively. If you follow a rusher, be deliberate. Sometimes, of course, you have to follow a lector who is also a trial lawyer, with a rich voice and magnificent diction, and then you can only be jealous.

One cannot think of delivery without including gestures, or (as it is getting to be called in more sophisticated circles) body language. In that respect, the very first syllable of body language is appearance. Not everybody can be monumental in physique or handsome in feature, but anybody can be neat. Anybody can stand straight and not slump or droop or twitch or squirm or rock. If you have a good sermon, it deserves a good frame, not gaudy but neat. Before you say a word with your lips, you are saying something merely with your appearance and your manner. It can help or it can hurt.

Gestures are the man. You have only to think of Maurice Chevalier who had but to tilt his straw hat, hunch his shoulders, raise one eyebrow, jut out that lower lip, and he established a mood. During the last century students were taught the Delsarte method of gesture, which was as formalized as that of the opera, with which, incidentally, he was originally connected. With him a gesture called for running your hand up the buttons of your vest, and when you reached the last button, you swept outward with a kind of effeminate flick of the fingers. This latter was "the soul" of the gesture. I hope Delsarte is in heaven. I am glad his system has left the earth.

Let's face it: some of us are stiff as railway semaphores; a few fortunate others are graceful in a natural masculine way, like the rhythmic wings of an eagle. I knew a priest whose speaking personality changed with the language he was using. In English he was as wooden as a lumberyard in his manner, and almost straight as a clothesline in his tones. But in the seminary he had studied Italian, and when he preached in that language, he was a waving and crackling fire. Wasn't it W. Somerset Maugham who said that there was more genuine acting in one Italian café than on the whole English-speaking stage?

Looking back, it seems to me that the men who were in the plays staged at our minor and major seminaries turned out to be the best preachers, undoubtedly because of this practice and of exposure to an audience. Later our entertainment took the passive form of movies. This was a sorry change.

Some have claimed there has been a change in public speaking in recent years, because while the medium of radio supposedly eliminated gestures, television has restored them. Just a quaint conceit, I reckon. There comes to mind, though, the memory of a tall, ruggedly handsome Redemptorist who was preaching a mission in a prison. At the end, one diminutive convict, whom he had noticed in the front row every night, came up to him and said, "You know, Father, you won't believe this, but I'm no Catholic, and the only reason I came each night was to watch your gestures. Out there on the street I was a pickpocket, and I was always imagining what I could do if I had your long, rangy fingers!" He spoke truer than he knew, because Father Mike Brennan was an accredited member of the National Society of Magicians (or whatever their official title is) and often entertained us with sleights of hand that had our eyes popping.

You perhaps have noticed that I have talked all around gestures rather than about them. Well, it comes back to the beginning: gestures are the man; to each his own. Only, remember: what might be natural to you may look ungainly or crude, or, on the other hand, cute or dainty. Ask someone to watch you and comment. But never ask a sincere friend for his opinion unless you can withstand a blunt surprise. He may even tell you that you look like a windmill.

167

We all tend to pick up mannerisms. Perhaps we shake our heads like a woodpecker for emphasis. Perhaps we "saw the air" with some favorite gesture far too often. But if a gesture comes instinctively with the thought, let it be. It is whole continents better than just standing there with your hands clasped before you, or with your fingers locked as if in pious prayer. We should pray *before* we preach.

The sensible approach to possible idiosyncrasies is to ask a friend to eavesdrop and, even more important, to "eye-drop" on you and point out any peculiarities. In stance it may be the rigidity of a statue or it may be the measured sway of a metronome. In speech it may be drawling or drooping or jamming phrases together or whatever. A tape recorder would play back the latter, but we might not detect it. We would have known what we intended to say, so to us it would be perfectly clear. But a stranger, coming in cold, would have no clues. However, for this delicate job, get a firm friend, not a honeyed flatterer.

One last thing. Eye contact with the audience is, of course, the ideal. It can be achieved only if you know your material thoroughly and are now wholly concerned with delivering it to the hearers. Here the true orator, that rare bird, himself reacts to the reactions of the audience. However, many competent speakers find that looking directly at the congregation distracts them, so they look just above them, or beyond the last benches. If the eyes then move in a natural semicircle, sweeping the church, this has almost the same effect.

If you read anything from the pulpit, whether it be the Gospel or a letter from the chancery, the elocution authorities maintain that your eyes should be *off* the printed page ninety percent of the time. That would demand at least a smidgeon of preparation. But it would avoid some weird mistakes. I knew an old priest from across the sea who read, "On Monday evening at eight there will be bingo in the school hall. Boom! Boom!" He had turned the pastor's exhortatory parenthesis into a double explosion.

25 ● Delivering the Good

To this ingrained and avowed Red Sox fan, the word "delivery" suggests a pitcher. But can you imagine the pitcher gripping the ball and not knowing how to throw it? This is the absurd parallel of a preacher who has on his desk or in his head a fine sermon, but does not know how to present it. Thinking, writing, memorizing (the latter at least to some degree) may load the rifle, but only delivery fires it.

Ideally, delivery takes the typed words, the little black paragraphs, and sends them out garbed in the bright costumes of animation, fervor, conviction, unction, inner glow. It makes the sleeping lines come alive.

Everyone has heard the hallowed yarn contrasting the actor with the preacher. "Why," the clergyman wanted to know, "do you move people, and we do not?" The actor is supposed to have responded, as he plucked off a false eyebrow, "Because we on the stage deliver fiction as if it were truth, while you in the pulpit offer truth as if it were fiction."

This, to be sure, is the ocean floor of oversimplification, conveniently forgetting the actor's advantages of vivid scenery, soft lighting, dramatic dialogue, crescendoing plot and a few other pluses. But the implication is that the actor pretends magnificently, while the preacher, with all his deep sincerity, projects miserably.

In other words, the man in the pulpit needs more than sincerity. Sincerity, like ordination, is presumed. You just start from there. If the preacher is not a saint whose sanctity shows and

169

glows, mere sincerity (strange phrase, that) can bore people to death. No matter how earnest a man may be, how dedicated or how virtuous, if he should drone along in deadly dullness, or if he should scream and roar till the very arches groan, he will only turn people off. Not even holiness covers a multitude of din.

I knew a priest once who, it seemed to me, was a saint in everything but official canonization. I was stationed in the same rectory with him for several years. I saw the hours he spent in chapel. I was awed by the rigorous, penitential life he lived, not in pious spurts but week after week, year after year. No hermit in the early desert was harder on himself.

Many times I heard him preach. By the end of the first sentence he was so fired with his theme that his voice leaped to a kind of strident shout. From then on it was like tying down the shrill whistle of a locomotive. The volume and the pitch funneled into your ears with the intensity of a siren, sustained right up to the last screaming "Amen."

I watched his listeners squirm and look helplessly around and pray he would stop. Meanwhile, he went on shouting out the truths for which I know he would be willing to come down from that pulpit and lay his head on the executioner's block and die. He was sincere unto death.

It is one of life's little ironies that a man like John Barrymore, hardly reputed as an ascetic, were he draped in a monk's habit and preaching in that pulpit, could send the same congregation out of church trembling for their salvation or seeking a general confession.

Don't get me wrong. It's a million times better to be a good priest than to be just a good preacher. It is also true that if people know the sanctity of a man's personal life, they will make huge allowances in other areas. But this does not disprove the modest reflection that sincerity alone is not enough. The holiest man can be a homiletic anesthetic.

That fanciful John Barrymore *tour de force* could happen once, but it could not be repeated often with the same congregation. They have a sixth sense about such things. They know that at the opposite end of the world from the sincere man without oratorical skill lives the skilled pulpit orator without sincere dedication. He is the preacher that the audience admires, but does not quite accept. They sense he is preaching himself rather than Jesus Christ. They feel that high up on the list of his admirers is his own not-too-shy self. They listen as they might listen to an organ concert, marveling at the virtuoso whose fingers sweep the keys and pull the stops. But he does not touch their lives. He does not get inside their hearts. He creates the impression not of a prophet rushing down from the hills with a message from God, but only of a performer with an ecclesiastical program. The artificial quaver, the breathy, guttural rasp, the sudden drop from the top of the scale to the deep basso depths, unless genuine emotion produce them, are pathetically phony.

Even genuine emotion can come out strange. It may be *natural to me*, but not normal. Sincerity and zeal are spirited horses and call for a disciplined rider. Dare to tape your talk and listen.

Possibly the most tragic mistake a preacher can make is to model himself on somebody else. You have to march with your own stride and to your own drum. Learn from everybody, but don't imitate anybody. Is there anything more pathetic than to see and hear a cheap plastic model of Archbishop Fulton Sheen? When young David buckled on Saul's armor, he walked clumsily, like a robot. Any strength he may have had was locked up in that oversized metal suit so he could not even swing the sword. But with his own weapons, the stones and the sling, and the grace of God behind him, he dropped the giant like a redwood tree.

Except on rare occasions, most of us do not hear many other priests preach, for one toweringly obvious reason: we usually are all preaching at the same time. (For that matter, most National League third basemen don't see American League third basemen at work either.) There is radio, to be sure, and TV, and extraordinary celebrations, but by and large, and considering all

171

the homilies preached, we rarely hear sermons by others. Most busmen don't climb aboard other buses, unless they have to; and a gravedigger is not enthusiastic about burying an elephant on his day off. Yet, if we did listen more often to other preachers, we undoubtedly would learn a little and perhaps a lot. Some would surprise us with their lucid and vivid presentation. From others we might become painfully aware about a certain grating flaw in our own delivery.

The psychologists claim that most of the good preachers are extroverts. I tend to agree with that because quite recently our community had one of those evaluating sessions with questionnaires, etc., and both the people conducting the tests and the community agreed that I was an introvert.

Certainly, I envy the priest with a personality like a skyful of stars who bubbles geniality and wears a smile as unconsciously as a hair comb. He drops into a group and makes fascinating conversation, lacing it with hilarious stories and droll dialects. And he does it so naturally, seemingly unaware that he is a social Fourth of July sparkler.

We introverts would never get anywhere in preaching except for two things. First, we have the opportunity of the silent, receptive audience. They are not talking about a thousand bits of trivia. You do not have to be louder or funnier than anyone else. The church silence is a nice sheet of white paper and all you have to do is write the message.

The second factor is that presumably you have prepared, and you know just what your message is. So, you don't have to be a world-beater or handsome or witty or magnetic. Just prepared. A homiletic Boy Scout.

Not that I am whittling away one sliver from the monumental advantage of the gifted extrovert. If the charming raconteur, the man who naturally dominates little social gatherings and has them laughing or leaning forward with absorbed attention, if he also prepares his sermons, he will leave far behind the plodding introvert. But God seems to balance things, for the extrovert is less likely to heft on his back the heavy sack of preparation, while the less freewheeling and less charismatic introvert almost automatically bends his back. The sky rocket and the traffic light have each their use, but almost never the twain meet.

Although few among us will have distinctive color and glitter in our conversation, most of us will at least be *natural* in our conversational tones. Nobody hits the wrong notes as he murmurs, "Please pass the parsnips," or when he shouts, "Throw out the lifeline!" However, that same man may find his tones streaking out in all kinds of weird directions when he speaks in public. No mystery to this at all, because when we speak in public:

1. We are speaking not to friends but to an anonymous crowd.
2. We are not within the cozy walls of a living room but in the alarming dimensions of a church or hall.
3. We are not talking in the usual casual phrases and colloquial rhythms of ordinary conversation but in the formal flow of structured sentences.
4. We therefore have to speak more slowly and more loudly than our normal wont.

This is what separates good preachers from poor ones: the ability to transpose the naturalness of ordinary conversation to the utterly different tempo and volume of the pulpit. It demands the actor's sense of timing and resonance and pause. It is the orator's instinctive communication with his audience.

Some preachers look out upon the rows and rows of lifted heads and meet the challenge by becoming pompous. Their throat towers up like a cathedral spire. The tones float out, orotund, bell-shaped, like a conscious trumpet solo. Sometimes they shift gears into a patented ministerial singsong, always, though, saving the best whine for the last. But it is the old story: they are affected, and no good is effected.

Far more common, though, is the fault of slurred and sloppy

diction. Perhaps, having been born in Brooklyn (my heart is buried under the pitcher's mound at what used to be Ebbett's Field), I am exceptionally sensitive to weird vowel quantities. In Brooklyn we used to *tawk* and *wawk* and write with *chawk*. No bird ever flew in Brooklyn; but it wasn't a *boid* either. The delicate nuance lies somewhere between. In England they used to say that the different noises they made served to separate the classes — or *clahses*, as they pronounce it.

But far beyond the borders of the Greatest City's Greatest Borough goes the tendency to blur the word endings. Lazy lips say *tuh* for "to," *fer* for "for," *yer* for "your." They say *goin', seein', human bein'. Doncha* (for "don't you"), *woncha* (for "won't you"), *histry* and *jography* (for "history" and "geography"), *gennelly* (for "generally"), *ahr* (for "our"), *jeet* (for "did you eat") and *hoozyer fren* (for "who is your friend"). The list is long and sad, and in some ways we all offend.

Almost as universal as original sin is that other tendency to drop the final syllable. In oratory this is "the fall." Many a speaker lets those endings drop as if he were a long-distance runner collapsing at the tape. Haven't you yourself, sitting in the audience, felt frustrated and irritated, straining to catch a swallowed word? Should you not perhaps wonder, "Do I do this, too?"

Often the last words in a sentence are the most important words in your argument, or the most touching words in your appeal — why then should they be the weakest in your delivery? Why swallow the clincher? The humble preacher should swallow nothing but his pride. Everything else he should project, round and clear, not muffled, not nasal, not metallic, not harsh, not in a lion's loud roar and not in a sheep's faint bleat, not in the machine-gun staccato and not in yawning drawl, but in the smooth, velvet, perfect way that you and I do it. Right?

At least we think we do it that way, but have you ever listened to yourself on tape? Anyone who has, and is pleased with the product, has to have a standard of excellence that needs to be jacked up. Most of us want to jump out the nearest window. In the first place, we do not recognize our own voice. "That's not *me!*" But it is. The fact is not flattering — just a fact — that when we speak we hear ourselves through *bone conduction*, and from *inside* the "shell" of our skull. As a result, our voice will sound *to us* much more resonant in quality and deeper in tone than it actually is. But to hear our voice *from outside* (as from a machine) is something else.

But the tape is you — or I, as we sound to others. It not only will reveal the quality of our voice (more Woolworth than the Tiffany we had supposed), but it will also probably wheel in a battery of floodlights to illuminate some glaring faults. Slovenly diction, swallowed endings, weird pauses, rapid-fire phrasings — when you stand on the sidelines the fumbles stand out.

Most people are surprised — and saddened — by the dullness of their delivery. G. B. Shaw pointed out, "There are fifty ways of saying *Yes*, and five hundred ways of saying *No*, but only one way of writing them down." Delivery is the art of taking those dead words on the page and giving them wings. But some of us have all the vivacity of a sick cow.

There was once a priest who received a tape recorder as a Christmas present. (I shall not even hazard the possibility that someone out there in the pews was delicately trying to tell him something.) The priest was delighted, and the very next Sunday he recorded his homily. Late that afternoon, after the babies had been baptized and the collections had been counted, he sat down to listen to himself. After the initial amazement of hearing this stranger deliver *his* sermon, he turned his attention to the message. But not for long. Later he said he knew the time when he awoke, but he could not say exactly when he fell asleep.

This frightened him, even conceding that the little man had had a busy day. After that, he still had the stalwart courage to listen to himself; only now he used to do it on a weekday afternoon in the empty church. He would put the recorder in the pulpit, next to the mike, take his seat in one of the rear pews and "take it" the way the people had to.

It changed his whole attitude toward preaching. What he said, and how he said it, began to improve in seven-league strides.

Radio and television have accustomed people to far higher standards of public speaking than we had in the past. These media personalities seem to wear their rich and fruity voices like boutonnieres, and carve their syllables like Greek statues. They have all attended schools for public speaking. They are professionals, and elocution is their life. (Who was the little boy who defined elocution as a way to put people to death while they were sitting down?)

Anyway, professional radio and TV are what people are constantly hearing. This is the competition. This is why the congregation, justly or unjustly, expects something like the same in our public speaking. Taking stock of our limited time and lack of training, it would be absurd to hope for perfection. But is there one of us who can't do better?

One annoying habit we can all drop (if by chance we have it) is not to stumble and stutter, "Er . . . uh . . . ah." Instead, just pause. It is better for you and for them.

Technical errors apart (like blurred diction and poor phrasing), the cancer of delivery is monotony. This lays the old ether cone over the face of any sermon. *Variety* is the spice of almost anything. Take up a national magazine and look at the ads. At the type, that is, not the pictures. (Perhaps some of the pictures were better not looked at.) Notice the four or five different kinds of type used in the advertisement. Imagine the text in the same type all the way through, and see how it loses.

The same is true of delivery. Repetition of the same tones and pace and inflection, breeds boredom. You do not find this sameness in children. Their tones and gestures are naturally vivacious and varied. Civilization, and its illegitimate son, human respect, have not as yet influenced them with the discipline that often becomes dullness.

But if we preachers speak about the Last Judgment,

shouldn't the emotion of fear tremble in our very tones? And if our theme is vice, shouldn't anger (at the sin, not the sinner) quiver in our voices? Shouldn't the mercy of God ride forth on notes of gratitude, and His majesty, on awe? Shouldn't the sounds follow the sense in oratory, as form follows function in architecture?

Wesley, as popular a preacher perhaps as ever lived (considering there was no radio or television in his day) said about his pulpit delivery, "I set myself on fire, and people come to watch me burn."

Of course it can be overdone, and has been. It brings to mind the STD on the seminary staff who was introduced at a Communion breakfast (remember those in yesteryear?) as the Professor of *Dramatic* Theology. On the other hand, perhaps theology should be dramatic.

Most of us fail in the other direction. One of the most gifted priests I ever knew (naturally he was a fellow Redemptorist) had a computer brain, a voice like a mellow cello, a story-telling ability that made the pictures on the wall lean a bit forward in their frames — and yet he was a mediocre speaker. I suspect that he had such a reputation for wit that he was determined he would not get the reputation of being a pulpit comedian. As a result, he was painfully formal, punctiliously dignified and absolutely dull. He bent too far the other way.

Hamlet marveled at the actor in the play when he saw tears sliding down the player's face. "What is Hecuba to him, or he to Hecuba, that he should weep for her?" And Hamlet went on to groan that he himself had such real reasons to weep. Nobody expects tears; but most of us, I fear, have laid away our emotions in the mummy case of pulpit propriety.

At least we can pay a little more attention to coloring our words, that is, to giving them the rolling value they should have and which they perhaps rarely receive. Whole semesters are devoted in elocution courses to emphasis achieved by a change of volume, or by a change of pitch, or by that powerful space bar on the typewriter of speech, the pause. For that matter, some instructors (and far be it from ignorant and unexperienced me to gainsay them) spend an introductory month teaching the speaker the proper way to breathe. From the diaphragm, Demosthenes, but please be conscious of it only in practice. Otherwise, like a too-studied golf swing, you attain only paralysis through analysis.

Then there is color. I recall not too long ago seeing Charlie Chaplin on television after the ceremony in which he had been knighted. "How was it?" the brash American reporter wanted to know. Sir Charles blinked from his wheelchair, a feeble eighty-five, and after a deliberate pause, answered, "It was very IM-PRESS-IVE." And the way he said it, you could believe it.

My skin still creeps when I recall what a radio engineer said to me about one of his bosses, who had for the time ousted our novena program from the air. "Father, let me tell you straight. He is an EE-VILL MAN." He spoke those two words so deliberately, dunking each syllable in deadly poison, that I gulped. It was like watching a man stick pins into a voodoo doll.

To some people, this sense of atmosphere comes naturally. They are the Sir Henry Irvings and Sarah Bernhardts who never made the stage. But the rest of us can at least learn from them. They have the trick of tossing a hook into a word and hanging on to it: words like "blood" and "wound" and "king."

With the usual rare exceptions, delivery has little to do with what you look like. A distinguished profile, an imperial carriage is fine, but after the first few sentences they want to know what you have to say. The speaker who impressed me most (and by sheer survival I have listened to lots of them) was the least prepossessing of any. To be very frank, he looked like a short, curiously wrinkled Boy Scout. (Actually he was a colonel in the United States Army.) His name was Carlos Romulo and I sat in the middle of the town auditorium in Norwood, Massachusetts, as he was telling us about General MacArthur and the Philippines, which he had just left.

His voice was a few rungs under ordinary. But with vivid word pictures, quivering but patently genuine emotion, and, above all, a spark-like leap of rapport between himself and the audience, he held us enthralled. I cite one detail. His very mediocre voice went momentarily hoarse. He took the glass of water from the stage table, raised it to his lips, and on second thought, poured half of it on the floor. In the silence, you could hear the splash. Then he went on, "This water means nothing to you." Then, in almost a whisper, "But where I just came from, men are dying . . . dying . . . for THIS!"

On the other hand (who was the Irishman, who after too many of these "on the other hand's" pleaded "For heaven's sake, stick to one hand!"), a fine imposing appearance is by no means a liability. However, from such a handsome envelope they expect a correspondingly impressive message. Whereas, if someone with the foreshortened architecture of myself (not tall enough to be gauntly Gothic, nor well-rounded enough to be plumply Romanesque) appears, he has at least this in his favor: they are not expecting much. If they can hear you, they are pleased. If you make any sense, they are a mite surprised. And if you happen to stumble upon saying something that is even a bit striking, they are amazed and delighted. They did not expect *that* from *this*. It evens out.

26 ● Down Memory Lane?

Honed to its finest edge, basic instruction on sermonizing might come down to this:

Assemble your materials. (Which means you have to *read* and *think*.)

Arrange your material. (Which means you have to *write*.)

Absorb your material. (Which means you have to *memorize*.)

It is the last requirement that makes the sparks fly.

Like the man who had no trouble at all giving up smoking (he had given it up dozens of times already) some priests have no trouble mastering their sermons. They bring the manuscript to the pulpit and read it. When such a preacher marches across the sanctuary to the pulpit with the large-type pages of some homily service in his confident hands, only one unspoken question runs along the rows of pews, "How well will he read it today?" After Mass some acerbic anticlerical may fling his venom-dipped dart, "We don't have a preacher. We have a Christian Science Reader."

Perhaps such a non-preacher or pulpit occupant may vigorously counter that popes and presidents and prime ministers read their addresses — so what, precisely, is wrong about reading a carefully prepared sermon? (Pass over the tiny detail that if it came from a homily service, someone else did the preparing. Maybe he figures that if the postman delivered it first, why should it be delivered again? Won't reading it suffice?)

However, that cleric must suffer from elephantiasis of the ego who blandly puts himself in the same lofty bracket as heads of State or Church. Does he really believe that the wire services are poised to snap up his every syllable? In his case will a conspicuous error of fact or a startling change of view hit the headlines or flash on the TV screen's eleven o'clock news?

The danger of being misquoted is perhaps the weakest of all possible arguments to justify the average priest in reading the average sermon. The strongest objection against reading is that from the moment you have started reading the talk, you have left a large portion of your audience behind. You will never hear it, but from the disappointed congregation there goes up a collective secret groan. Between you and them, your manuscript rises like the Great Wall of China. Or at least it is like the grill between visitor and convict in the reception room of the prison. Surely, psychologically it poses a barrier to full and easy communication. In a vote by the listeners, between preaching and reading, preaching would win by a landslide.

The material sent out by the homily services is meant to be just that: material. It is an aid to write a sermon, not a substitute to replace one. We are supposed to borrow a bit from the homily aid, and borrow a bit from other sources, and weave all the strands into our own pattern for our own rug. Who wants to be the echo of another's voice, or the ventriloquist's dummy sitting on some remote cassocked lap?

To this rule of "never reading," there are, to be sure, exceptions. And that is precisely what they are: exceptions. If you are preaching, for example, on contraception and want the audience to realize that what you say is no mere personal opinion but comes from the Vicar of Christ himself, it is not only lawful but laudable to read a paragraph or so, and, in fact, to make it very plain that you *are* reading. In fact any time, so long as you read only a passage, the reading of a few lines can lend at once both variety and authority. (Or, as one of our grand old ushers would say, "author-iety.")

When I opt for at least some memorizing, I am thinking in terms of the ten-minute or fifteen-minute talk. You could hardly blame Cardinal Newman for reading his sermons, because they go on for page after page after page, as you know from his works. But he was one of the giants of English prose and offered sentences that were like long, winding, shining rivers, and whose very structure demanded reading. No man spoke the way he wrote.

On the few occasions when he did venture to speak without a manuscript he was frankly and almost cruelly assessed as being "incoherent, rambling, wearisome, deplorable." But set his prepared copy before him, let him clear his throat, and he could fill the chapel and fascinate his hearers.

I am under the impression that he preached seated in a sanctuary chair. Personally I have rarely done this (perhaps occasionally in a convent) because I was always conscious that in the operating room the surgeon stood up. It was the anesthetist (whose job it was to keep the patient asleep) who sat down. And then quite recently I read, or at least I noted what I had often read and never realized, that our Lord Himself *sat* in Peter's boat when He preached to the crowd along the shore. Water is a fine conductor, I imagine, but that must have been a gloriously rich and resonant voice pouring from a seated preacher.

But we were speaking about memorizing. Cardinals (like Newman) and presidents and popes aside, the rest of us must face the problem of getting our talks into our heads. We have to do some memorizing. Many memorize only a sketch. Some preachers would be handcuffed if they did more. I have known talented preachers who could write superbly. They could make words ring bells and jump through hoops, but when they attempted rigid word-for-word memory it laced them up in an oratorical straitjacket.

These men hardly memorized at all, at most probably only an outline; but when they took their stand in the pulpit, they had behind them a reserve of diligent preparation, and they had within them God's own gifts of fluency and spontaneity — and the combination rose in a thundering, powerful wave.

For men like these I have something approaching awe, and something too close to jealousy. But on second thought there are not too many of these around.

Put me (if you will indulge the intrusion of the personal) at the other end of the street. For many years I memorized (or tried to) word for word. I still memorize sentence for sentence, or perhaps better put, idea after idea. For example, let me take a sentence at random (why should I lie to you?) from a little talk about "St. Joseph in the Land of St. Patrick." If the combination seems curious, remember there is only one day between their feasts, and if the Wednesday novena comes on the Seventeenth of March, and the parish is in an Irish barrio, you would be wise not to rouse sullen Celtic disappointment or Hibernian hard feelings by ignoring the Apostle of the Gael.

Anyway, suppose the manuscript says: "Let St. Joseph follow any quiet crooked Irish road, and it may not be long till he comes upon some patient, plodding donkey, the very braying image of the glossy beast that carried Mary that first Christmas Eve."

In the preaching, that road might come out twisted instead of crooked; the donkey might be trudging instead of plodding; his hide might have to settle for smooth or sleek; and Bethlehem might become "that first Christmas Eve."

In other words I try to memorize the picture. Interestingly enough, though, I find that when I repeat the same talk at the next novena service or the next Mass, I tend to say exactly what I said at the preceding one.

Practically every book on preaching that I have leafed through, hangs over memory's door a huge sign that reads, KEEP OUT! They don't go so far as to warn of ATTACK DOG ON THE PREMISES! but they leave no doubt about the prohibition. Each author lifts an admonishing finger and puts a paternal arm around your shoulder and whispers that none of the great preachers ever memorized. Frankly, I wonder. I also wonder if memorizing would have such a consistently bad press if it did not entail such grim hard work.

This, like the bishop's bad brother, is rarely brought up. What they do wave aloft is the charge that committing a sermon to memory is like laying it out in the casket of oratorical *rigor mortis*. No life, no freedom, no abandon, no spontaneity. A cardboard homily.

They hint that instead of the Dove of the Holy Spirit hovering over such a preacher, the parrot of slavish memory perches on his shoulder. The sentences come off the conveyor belt of memory without conviction or vitality or fire. Their poor preacher even has a faraway look in his eye as if he were scanning the lines on a distant page.

But isn't all this a robust rebuttal, not of memorizing, but of poor memorizing? If the talk has been *well* memorized, then all the speaker's personality can be channeled into his delivery. A native woman in the tropics, walking down the road with a bundle poised on her head, can meet a friend and chat and gesticulate as if the bundle were not there. In similar fashion, if the sermon is *in* our head, not on it, we can have the same freedom. Will anyone say that a good actor does not deliver his lines with warmth and color and the natural tones of life? But haven't his lines been memorized? Ask him. He'll show you the worn carpet he paced getting them down.

The man who does not memorize may find himself like a plane circling the field, repeating the same thought in practically the same boring words. The man who memorizes says something new in each sentence; he does not repeat. Who writes and speaks the same line twice?

To preachers who achieve their effect by the use of vivid words, apt comparisons, balanced sentences and, in general, what we call style — to them, memory is indispensable. Without the precise phrases the whole effect is lost. They have to bring to the pulpit what they composed at the desk. However, those

preachers whose forte is delivery (those rare gifts of natural eloquence, variety of tones, an actor's sense of timing, instinctive
rapport with the audience) will find memorizing less necessary,
because they depend not so much on the matter as on the manner. And that is always with them.

As we grow older, too, memory, like the hairline, tends to
recede. The mental adhesive begins to dry up. On the other hand,
a memory that has done its jogging by regular use all through
the years, does not lose its elasticity as quickly as one that has
rocked the years away in a lazy hammock. It should also be
brought out that it is far easier to memorize what you yourself
have just written. In that sense the very writing of a sermon is
the first step toward planting it in the memory.

For myself, I never now trust my memory completely. Time
was, in brash and self-assured youth, when I would. I mind well
(as my uncle used to say) that very first Christmas in the ministry. It was 1930, and the Midnight Mass was being broadcast.
Those were the days when radio was just getting out of its
rompers, and there was a standing microphone about as big as a
pie plate at the gates of the Communion rail. I took my place
behind it and delivered my talk. The next morning the pastor
told me how pleased he was. What pleased him, though, was not
the sermon, but the fact that his brother in a neighboring state
had phoned that he had heard the program. In those days the indoor sport was not listening, but "dialing for distance."

Anyway, what amazes me now is that I never had the slightest fear that my memory might fail. Today, after preaching
from a pulpit over the air almost every week for more than
thirty years, I would not dream of taking my place behind a mike
without at least a page of key sentences.

Why this mature diffidence, in contrast to the bold optimism
of confident youth? Because in the meantime I have come to
learn that a man's mind can go blank as an empty blackboard at
any moment. Some slight distraction like a baby's cry or a late-
comer swaggering down the aisle — and your train of thought

goes careening over the embankment. Or, for no reason at all, one of those delicate disks in the cranial computer slips just a silly little millimeter, and suddenly you do not know what you have just said. Or, comes the frightening thought: Have I just said what I am about to say? Perhaps being a senior citizen has a deal to do with it; but, like golf, it is a humblin' experience.

That is why I always bring a small sheet of notes into the pulpit. I can, at the very least, snatch a new thought and begin from there. Generally one glance at the notes restores one's confidence. To the pulpit mariner that page or that envelope or that card is a lifesaving compass which gives him an instant reading on his bearings. For myself, I may preach a half-dozen sermons without having to consult the notes; but it is always reassuring to know that, like a security blanket, they are there.

On more than one occasion I have heard people praise their pastor's preaching, not because of what he had said, but because he had never used a note. Never? No, never! But did his memory ever fail? I cattily surmise that if it did, he went right on talking. After years of sermonizing, it is conceivable that a preacher can throw his tongue on automatic pilot and just keep speaking. But should he just go on "batting," as the disparaging phrase has it? Is it not simpler for the preacher, and more profitable for the audience, if he just glances down at the sketch and gets back on the logical track?

To sum up: Though I am aware that I file a minority report, I am still stubborn enough to counsel any young priest to memorize his homilies practically word for word. The only valid objection (to my provincial and prejudiced eye) is that memorizing takes time and trouble. As to the time, perhaps we could borrow a little of that from our light and trivial reading. As to the trouble, every profession has its drudgery. Even a brain surgeon does not just excise the tumor. He has to scrub up before and sew up after.

Memorizing, alas, is an unappealing but indispensable task for the young preacher. Someday they may develop a process by which we press the manuscript against a mysteriously lubricated forehead, and by osmosis the contents will be immediately Xeroxed on the brain. Meanwhile, though . . .

Hard work? Of course it is. But be sure of this. Memory is never Love's Labor Lost. It is rather All's Well That Ends Well. And without it there might be A Comedy of Errors.

27 ● Radio and Television

Since my experience with television is minuscule (about a dozen stints at wide intervals), I am certainly not equipped to ladle out much klieg-light counsel. Frankly, the tube scares the tonsure off me. Perhaps that is part of our septuagenarian syndrome whereby we oldsters still look with awe at a lighted box whose steel-fingered antennae can reach up and claw out of the night air a football game on the West Coast and fling it in technicolor splendor into a living room. Meanwhile today's toddlers, brought up on Sesame Street, just take all this for granted.

At any rate, there should be only high praise for the young priest who uses the local TV station to give the Gospel the exposure it deserves. Nothing since the invention of printing has had such an impact on the mind of man as television. Not even the press exerts so vivid a thrust. One can only regret (and we can recognize many reasons for this and lament them all) that up to this point the Church has been unable to take advantage of the most powerful of all possible apostolates.

As far as the preacher is concerned, the major difficulty in television is that you have to know your talk thoroughly. In radio, you can, of course, read the sermon, though personally I have rarely done so. One reason is that good readers are rarer than good talkers. When a man has memorized his manuscript, at least to the extent of the consecutive ideas, the chances are better that he will fall into the natural rhythms and intonations of conversational speech in his delivery. But when a man reads, unless he has the actor's sense of variety and all its subtle nuances, he risks the danger of being artificial, monotonous and dull.

Better, it seems to me, the occasional stumblings and hesitations of a "spontaneous" (i.e., non-reading) delivery than the polished prose but mechanical projection of a parroted manuscript. Each method has its advantages and its drawbacks, but when you make *your choice,* don't overlook the fact that poor old human nature hates the work of memorizing. There is no question about which method is *easier*. The problem is which one is *better*.

But, there, we have wandered off into radio, and we had been discussing television. The obvious hazards of the latter are the hot lights (grin and bear it!), the cameras (everybody knows about little old red eye), and the fact that often your program will be "live." This means anything can happen, and according to Murphy's law, always does.

One Easter not long ago at a Mass in our diocesan TV center, a boy soprano in the front rank of the cassocked and surpliced choir fell over like a domino. Apparently the lights and the fasting had combined to send him into a faint. A couple of stagehands gently pulled the lad aside while the camera switched from the preacher (and the crumpled lad at his feet) to the red robes of His Eminence. They told me later, those at home, that they had not been aware of any mishap. I guess what you naturally do in a case like that, is just keep on talking, glad that you have done your best to prepare, and trusting in the Lord to see you through. You feel wobbly, but it turns out that nobody "out there" was the wiser.

With TV's sightless brother, radio, I am a bit better acquainted. If credentials have to come out, I have spoken almost a hundred times on national broadcasts, like NBC's old *Catholic Hour* and CBS's former *Church of the Air*. For more than thirty years, I have preached a weekly radio novena on a major Boston station. This is not to imply that I am good, but it should certify that I have served my time behind a mike.

One superb feature of a radio ministry is that a man can be as far from handsome as even I am, and the audience is blithely unconcerned. They presume you look somewhere between Cardinal Richelieu and Cary Grant. Of course when they do see you, their eyebrows may go up in pained unbelief, and their Adam's apple drop in a disappointed swallow; but an encounter like this you must learn to shrug off as casually as you would bankruptcy or infectious hepatitis.

I recall sauntering one evening through the booths of a mission exhibit and overhearing a lady say to her companion, "There goes Father Manton." And the other lady, who apparently listened regularly to our radio novena, just stared. Her chin dropped, and she murmured almost to herself, "Is *that* Father Manton?" I walked over and smiled apologetically. "Never mind, dear," I said. "God also made parsnips."

In the matter of radio delivery, there is only one slight difference from pulpit speech — at least only one that occurs to me. This is the matter of a faster tempo. There are two reasons for this. First, in a pulpit you sometimes have to calculate on your voice reaching the rear of the church, so your speaking has to be more deliberate. Secondly, when you are in a pulpit, there is your physical presence and incidental gestures, to occupy the attention of the listener. These, of course, are not there in a radio talk. Most speakers seem to sense this and almost naturally speak faster on the air. Don't rush, but don't ever drag: trippingly on the tongue, as old Will would have it.

The drawback here, though, is that with a slightly faster pace you may run out of material faster than you had anticipated. The prudent virgin always brings a little more oil for the radio lamp.

It goes without saying (but we shall say it anyway) that every radio sermon should be timed beforehand. A big radio station lives by the second hand on the clock. Einstein's theory of relativity used to be waggishly illustrated by the fact that for a swain courting his sweetheart, an hour passed like a minute; but to anyone rubbing up against a hot stove, a fraction of a second is like five minutes. On the radio, one minute of dead air is a long, long time. In broadcasting, silence is the only sin.

So, you should not finish before your specified time. Some radio speakers mark off on the margin of their manuscript two-minute intervals: 7:02, 7:04, 7:06, etc. Then they keep glancing at the clock to see that they are on schedule. Most men will just time the total speech in advance, and then mark off on the manuscript the last three minutes. When the clock shows this, they will lightly trapeze to that three-minute prepared conclusion. At first blush, you might think that such a procedure would fracture unity like a jigsaw puzzle; but apparently few logicians in the radio audience notice the disjunction.

If your radio sermon originates in a studio, try to think you are speaking to the engineer. (If he praises you, it is the ultimate accolade, for he is a weary automaton, alertly watching dials but rarely listening to the message.) This one-to-one communication is what radio was made for. However, if you are broadcasting from a pulpit, forget the radio audience and preach to those before you — only try to preach a mite faster than usual. Your listeners, especially the shut-ins, living in their narrow world of walls and windowpanes, relish the impression that they are sitting in a large church, hearing the sermon from a distant pew.

If you happen to have a regular weekly broadcast from a church, you will unconsciously -- or very consciously — keep your eye on the church clock; but actually it will amount to flying by the seat of your pants. Good old routine keeps you in the desired rut. But occasionally the unusual happens. I recall on one such occasion glancing down at my inexpensive electric watch and noting with horror that it had stopped cold. The church clock was shrouded with a Christmas holly wreath, and I could just about guess what it said. But God was with me, and I hit the landing runway just about on time. But after that I never wholly relied on the electric watch.

Like anything else, practice makes, if not perfect, at least reasonably accurate. If you speak for fourteen minutes week after week (not reading a manuscript — that is for the robots!) a kind of sixth sense of timing develops, possibly akin to the knack of the professional bartender who scorns the precise measuring jigger and pours by tilt and by splash. Isn't that the way our mothers used to cook?

28 ● Homiletic Hazards

In theory the earnest, inoffensive preacher should be as remote from harassment as the venerable portraits on the walls of an old-line gentlemen's club. In fact, however, anyone who has paid his dues in the preachers' union in the dull coin of routine experience can offer at least a six-pack and possibly even a wine cellar of incidents in rebuttal. You do not have to have paddled your pulpit canoe long, before you become aware that in the waters lurk unsuspected rocks and unnerving rapids.

Would you believe that one Sunday morning a hippie lass with stringy black hair and blue denim slacks suddenly leaped up from a front pew, hurled a Missalette and invited me to go to hell? She went striding down the side aisle, flinging back profane comments over her hunched shoulder. And I had been speaking on something as serene and uncontroversial as the love of our Blessed Lord as symbolized by His Sacred Heart!

How to react? You take a deep breath and try to pretend that nothing has happened. You talk to the opposite side of the church in deliberate measured tones as if the interruption had never occurred. The last thing you want is a tennis match of charge and defense, particularly when the other's think-box is likely to explode.

During World War II, I recall a soldier standing near the side door of our large church and suddenly shouting out, "You're a liar!" In those days we used to get almost fifteen hundred people for the novena in the upper church, and the preacher's voice also went downstairs via loudspeaker to at least a thousand more. I could feel the tenseness of the congregation, so I said in a playful vein, "Well, perhaps I am a liar, but really not in this particular instance." By that time the rector and a couple of burly ushers had piloted the soldier out the side door. When the cool night air hit him, he seemed to sober up and said, "I guess I've been through too much in the war. Too much stress and strain." The rector took one whiff and said, "Too much Haig and Haig!"

Another time someone roared out, "But what about divorce?" With a lightning prayer to the patron saint of mental reservation I said, "I was just coming to that." Whereupon one of my confreres, Father John Murphy, who was a huge tower of a man, looking like Goliath in a black cassock and a tinkling rosary, beckoned the interrupter out of the pew. The shouter rose to his own six-feet-four height and just scowled, as if to say, "Come and get me!" So Father Murphy swiftly shifted gears and said, "Don't you want to go to confession?" "Oh, of course, I want to go to confession." So Father Murphy led him down the long aisle and the first thing the man knew he was standing outside on the church steps. His brow clouded. "I'll never darken this church door again!" he said. "Can I have your word for that?" Father Murphy asked.

Sometimes the distraction in the pews is as silent as an Egyptian mummy but still utterly disconcerting. As I write this we have at our services a fine tall grenadier of a lad, an outpatient from the mental hospital down the street. We call him "The Windmill." All during the sermon he sits in the bench blessing himself. In a blurry perpetual circle he blesses himself with an ever-faster sign of the cross. Only in the winter when he wears a heavy overcoat does the pace slacken. Poor fellow, he reminds us all that if one of those tiny crimson capillary threads in *our* brain short-circuited, we would be no better.

As the years go on, we grow, I think, more tolerant. I recall many years ago one Lenten night, when the frozen grin of the young man in the third pew in that Staten Island church never stopped. I was tempted to pause and fire a well-aimed sarcastic

194

shot. But I made myself preach in the other direction, trying to forget. Afterwards, the pastor's first words were, "I meant to warn you about so-and-so. A great lad, but he has this affliction of a paralyzed face." God was with me that night.

Crying babies, of course, are the constant enemy. As in the case of the husband who forgets his wedding anniversary, nobody has ever come up with a satisfactory solution. One thing is certain: man has never yet built a cathedral that a determined baby cannot fill. Not only that, but some mothers seem to prefer to bring the youngster close to the loudspeaker, as if he needed that edge.

I have seen people in the vicinity glare at such a mother, and the mother glare witheringly back. She seems to be asking, "Don't you know the sacrifice I made to come to this Mass?" And the others' stony eyes are saying, "You make it impossible for anyone really to hear Mass!"

In those blessed churches that have a crying room, the problem dissolves like spring snow, and, like Abou Ben Adhem, may their tribe increase! But where there is no crying room, but only a crying need for one, and yet no lack of crying babies (though even one outraged little larynx is enough), my meek counsel is that you learn to cooperate with the unavoidable. If you lose your temper, you may lose many friends in the same sad explosion. You may end up regretting your outburst the rest of your life.

I know it is utterly unfair. You have prepared your sermon well; you feel you have a worthwhile message; you have so few opportunities to reach your flock — so why can't the mother take the child back to the vestibule, at least till the homily is over? I can't imagine any legal eagle wanting to soar up in defense of the contrary position. But I still feel that if you ask her to do this, even the people who are annoyed at the child's tantrum, would be more annoyed at your loss of temper. Once more quoting the king of Siam, "It is a puzzlement."

If you think a baby can derail the oratorical express, how about a dog? I have known a few pastors who, perhaps with a nod

195

in the direction of the stable of Bethlehem, said Mass while their Labrador retriever or German shepherd crouched in the corner of the sanctuary. Maybe a St. Bernard would be more appropriate.

But a dog padding down the aisles is, of course, instant death to all attention. The obvious commonsense solution is to keep the doors closed, unless you happen to be St. Francis. Once the canine congregation is inside, it is a persuasive usher who can quietly lead it out. Often an altar boy, with that natural boy-and-dog rapport, can lead the pooch past the pews and into the parking lot where it belongs.

The mention of a parking lot brings up the great or even middle-sized outdoors, where you may sometimes have to speak on the occasion of a field Mass, a cemetery ceremony, a Holy Name rally, a May procession. At least such were some of the alfresco events of former years. Nowadays your outdoor talk might take place at a demonstration, a protest march, or a mass meeting.

The hazards have not changed, only the atmosphere: the spiritual climate, that is, not the physical. A glaring sun, a whipping wind, driving clouds of dust — these assaulted William Jennings Bryan, and they still bear down on us. There is no solution. You just cope, as well as you can. Of course, if it is a small affair, as at a graveside in a cemetery, you can choose your spot to leeward so that the wind sweeps your voice toward your hearers.

One disadvantage to outdoor speaking, particularly if you are speaking into the teeth of a constant wind, can be a following laryngitis. Far be it from me to diagnose why, but I suspect it is because the throat has become warm, and the breezes pouring into it are cool, so you develop an inflammation. Trying to speak over a heavy cold can induce the same condition. Once, instead of doing the commonsense thing and quitting, I went on trying to speak at the Sunday Masses until finally I could not speak at all. The doctor told me my vocal cords were on the point of hemorrhage. When I missed my regular novena service that week, a kindly old lady (they take a proprietary interest in you after a few years) wanted to know why I was absent. I told her my vocal cords were in poor condition. She became very concerned and very confidential. "Oh, Father, that's too bad. Why don't you have them out?"

As far as the preacher is concerned, there are really only two important concerns in any church. Not whether the edifice is Gothic or Romanesque or Twentieth Century Practical. Ruskin had something when he observed that all architecture was but a glorified roof. What should interest the preacher is: (1) audibility and (2) temperature.

But why emboss the obvious? If people come to church in the winter (and traditionally they keep their overcoats on, though I never could see why) normal room temperature is much too warm, because you add to this the diffused body heat of a large congregation.

When people are either perspiring or shivering, they are not, to put it mildly, in ideal receptivity. More than anything else they perhaps want out. That thermostat is a tiny gadget, but unless you use it intelligently, you had better be a combination of Lacordaire and Bossuet to hold your audience. Keep your cool, and theirs!

As to the audibility, this is even more important. If you cannot be understood, the whole homily is a mockery. You do not have to be seen; the fact that a person is behind a pillar need be no serious detriment to a sermon's effect. In a sense it is like listening on the radio. At the basilica where I happen to be stationed, we had for many years such throngs at the novena that during three of the eight services the downstairs church would be crowded, too. The sermon went down there by loudspeaker, but there was a "live" Benediction. I always suspected that many preferred the lower church because it had perfect acoustics plus the sterling advantage that you did not have to look at the preacher.

Having come from the era when a public-address (or P.A.)

197

system in church was undreamed of, to that when it is taken for granted, I treasure a microphone as a modern miracle. During the thirties in our basilica the pulpit was far down the side aisle. You were told to aim your naked voice at the third confessional. There are six on each side, and in those days every weekend (Friday and Saturday) there would be long lines of penitents. You aimed your voice and you bellowed like a train announcer, competing with the whir and jangle of the trolleys that clacked and banged past the open doors.

With the forties came the mike and the P.A. outlets (they have gone from multicellular to columnar) and you could really try to preach instead of just shouting. But sound systems are many and different. Some of them are indifferent, some poor, some superb. All should be adjusted to the voice of the speaker. This is not being finicky. It is being sensible. Pastors have told me that men of towering oratorical talent, like Archbishop Fulton Sheen, have asked to try the microphone in the church before they spoke. They would, obviously, make allowance for an empty church; but it would give them the feel of the place and of the P.A. system.

I'll never forget one occasion when Cardinal Cushing (he was then only our auxiliary bishop) preached at our basilica. In those days he was in his physical prime and had a voice like twenty trumpets. As he spoke, I stood in the sacristy, and, unknown to him, turned down the volume to its lowest level. I did not want to turn off the power completely, lest he be offended. But even at that faint setting the poor needle would hit the other side of the dial and bounce back as if it had been punched.

Someone in the sacristy had made a record of the talk. I asked for it and sent it to him. We met about a week later at a banquet. I asked him how he liked the record. "Aw, Joe, I sounded like a fish-peddler!" The marvelous thing is that ever after, when Cardinal Cushing spoke in the basilica, he toned down as much as he could tone down (meaning that the .45 caliber became a .38) because he had developed a decent respect for our microphone. But as the years went on he seemed to fear no others.

Take him all in all, he was a magnificent man, but I should not wonder if at the last day his piercing tones get the call over Gabriel for waking the dead.

Some Suggestions
for Sermon Patterns

Like different pans for different cookie patterns, the imaginative preacher has at arm's reach different sermon forms into which he can pour his homiletic mix. Is this necessary? From one viewpoint, surely. Most of us face the same people Sunday after Sunday, and if want to lasso their straying attention, our approach had better wear different hats — to mangle a metaphor (which is another way of getting attention).

The pulpit is not alone with this problem. Dick Young, a sportswriter (of all people) writing for the *New York Daily News* (of all papers) set it down bluntly for young reporters; but it applies just as trenchantly to young priests, and, if you can imagine such a thing, even to older ones. The parentheses are mine:

1. *Tell it.* (Just *it.* Don't wander.)
2. *Tell it right.* (Be accurate. Every homily is *not* entitled to one heresy.)
3. *Tell it well.* (If the package isn't attractive, the shopper will pass it by.)
4. *Tell it differently the next day.* (The next day means a new ball game with a different lead. For the preacher the next Sunday means a new sermon with the same audience, so it calls for a new treatment.)

To meet this challenge, there follow here a few different possible treatments or plans or patterns for sermons. None is original. They are the same old saddles that "pulpit war-horses" have worn for years untold. If you feel comfortable on any or several of them, good luck! They have carried some great riders in their day.

1 — The Echo

This gets its power from the repetition of a phrase which booms like a solemn gong at the end of each paragraph. It uses the same technique as the ballade in poetry. Remember Chesterton's reluctant suicide who at the end of every stanza decides, "I think I will not hang myself today," because he has not yet read the works of Juvenal, or tomorrow is payday, or this or that, and so on . . .?

For the preacher, the refrain phrase will grow naturally out of the topic. Suppose his theme is the incident of David and Bathsheba. You remember how Nathan the Prophet tells King David his parable about the rich man with all his possessions who still stole the poor man's sole treasure, his little ewe lamb. And King David roars, "Show me that man! He is worthy of death!" And Nathan looks him levelly in the eye and says, *"Thou art that man!"*

So now the preacher could go on to describe a man who is a model in his own parish, but when he goes off on vacation, abandons his conscience at the airline terminal. He breaks the commandments like peanut brittle. After all, it is summer and he is far from home. And then — the echo: Does your conscience point its long accusing finger and say, *"Thou art that man!"*

Another paragraph might be the padded expense account, and another the inflated insurance claim, and another the cold abandonment of a father or mother in a nursing home, or the reading of cruddy paperbacks while conning oneself into believing, "These don't affect me," and so on. But at the end of each, the echo: Does your conscience stride across the floor of your soul, point its finger and say, *"Thou art that man!"*

Orators have been using this echo effect since Cicero was in knee pants or at least in a tot's toga. Notice that the effect of the echo chamber is multiplied when the refrain is a question.

Suppose, for instance, you are speaking on devotion to our Lady. You regret, to your audience, that ever since Vatican II the rumor (not the fact!) has gone around that the Church, very quietly, but very really, has been downgrading devotion to Mary. So you try the echo approach:

The Second Vatican Council was convened on the feast of Mary's Maternity and was concluded on the feast of Mary's Immaculate Conception. Does that sound like downgrading?

No council in history gave more time to our Lady in its discussion, or more space to her in its documentation. Does this sound like downgrading?

When the council ended, it restated two towering truths: (1) That Mary was the Mother of God, and (2) as such, she was the first of all creatures. Does this sound like downgrading?

The pope who opened the council, John XXIII, left Rome only once in his pontificate, to visit our Lady's shrine at Loretto. Does this sound like downgrading?

The pope who closed the council, Paul VI, on the last day of the third session, gave orders to the Sistine Choir to sing hymns to Mary for a half hour before the final Mass. As concelebrants at that Mass, he personally designated the bishops of our Lady's famous shrines, like Lourdes and Fatima and LaSalette and Guadalupe. Does this sound like downgrading?

The council was hardly over when Pope Paul went to Fatima to present to that shrine the Golden Rose. A few months later, he traveled eastward to Mary's shrine at Ephesus. And that same year, on December 8, when Rome was chilly and rainy and he himself had a racking cold, he laid a bouquet at Mary's statue by the Spanish steps. Does that sound like downgrading?

And the conclusion would point out that when you want to know the official stance of the Catholic Church toward Mary, you do not go to some callow curate, more eager at the moment to make *Time* than *The Book of Life,* or to some nun, a bit intoxicated with her new freedom, but to the pope and the council. *And with them, there is no downgrading!* Rather, there is an uplifting example of official dedication and personal devotion.

II — Problem and Solution

To explain the meaning of this sermon plan would be to paint the obvious in tall white letters on the side of a cliff. Yet it does call for a cautionary suggestion. In preaching a sermon which first outlines the problem and then offers a solution, the general tendency is to beat the problem to death and then come gasping in with a solution in the last two minutes. Most logical listeners would prefer their homiletic Martini with a different proportion, say just a wee drop of problem and a generous dash of solution. Or, to put it another way, they will cheerfully grant the diagnosis. They want you to get on to the prescription, the remedy.

If, for example, we were to speak on the problem of pain (and he is a brave man who does), how easy it is to line up the wheelchairs, count the white canes, walk down the hospital wards, and, in brief, survey the world's vast miles of misery. But people need only be nudged about the presence of pain among them. They know, of their own grim experience, how thorny life can be. What they seek is comfort and courage and motives to carry their cross with patience, rather than to drag it with bitter reluctance.

Far better than repeating the too well-known lurid litany of suffering would be to remind our hearers that *we* see life only from the short-range view of a few years, while God has the advantage of seeing our life from the mountain peak of eternity. While we do not know the answer to the problem of pain, we do know the solid fact that God loves us. If He strikes us, it has to be for a good reason, just as the lifesaver may strike a struggling swimmer to knock him out and save him. Our suffering comes from the hand of Christ, a hand whose jagged red hole tells how much love He holds for us.

So, if it is true that "nobody knows the trouble Ah's seen," then the preacher must set down as his goal, not to paint a giant mural featuring trouble and all its tribes, but to cite magnificent instances of quiet heroism in people who have looked eyeball to eyeball at trouble or even tragedy, and have either gallantly conquered it or serenely endured it.

The absurdity of showcasing *the problem* becomes manifest if the problem is, for instance, "bad books." To dwell on that evil would be to exploit it. It should take but a sentence or two to hang up the dartboard target of so much permissive pornography, and then spend the rest of the time hurling the pointed darts. The points could be the pathetic effects of such reading, from the woeful waste of time, to the enriching of the scoundrels who write the stuff, to the dumping of moral garbage on the floor of one's intelligence, and the dirty, cobwebby memories that may stay for years in the attic of our minds.

In contrast, take a rather abstract theme like envy. The plan might be as simple as this:

THE PROBLEM

A new personality comes into our little corner of the world. That corner may be an office, a school, a hospital, even a church choir. Said individual may be more handsome than we, or more wealthy, or more talented, or more personable. The tendency is to be jealous, to envy.

THE SOLUTION

To remind yourself that: (1) Envy is the only vice that does the sinner no good. If you rob your neighbor's wallet, you have his money. If you spread slander, you have the satisfaction that other people may look down upon him. But when you envy, it does him no harm and you no good. (2) Envy does not harm your "enemy." Probably he or she does not even know that your envy or jealousy even exists. It is the sin of the stupid, because all it does is hurt you, the one who practices it. (3) Often we would not envy if we knew the whole story. Things are seldom completely what they seem. Ask any doctor, lawyer, priest. (4) Envy is so low a failing that nobody ever boasts of it. Drunkards boast of hangovers, libertines of conquests; but nobody ever boasted of being jealous.

Why "eat your heart out," when it is only going to give you moral indigestion? "Love your neighbor" and you will not envy him for a gift he got from God.

III — Surprise Opening, With Instances

As you have already noticed, or shortly will, some of these suggested sermon plans overlap. They differ only about where you put the emphasis. In this third model, the emphasis is on the introduction, which should be arresting, in the sense of challenging the attention at once. For this reason, it should be preceded by a measurable pause, in order to give a background of silence to the unusual beginning.

Thus, if you were speaking on the *Fifth Commandment,* and wanted to stress the immorality of dangerous driving (a much more common violation than shooting with a "Saturday-Night Special"), you might sketch out a plan like this:

DANGEROUS DRIVING

1. Everyone knows about the overcrowded housing situation; but did you know that our *cemeteries* are becoming overcrowded? Not exactly a flight to the suburbs, but some cemeteries do not have accommodations for new applicants.

2. One answer might be cremation. But a better answer is to stop dying. This sounds absurd? It isn't absurd at all if you limit it to the young, and ask them to stop dying. Did you know that drinking and driving is the major cause of death among the young?
3. Did you know that when the legal drinking age was lowered to eighteen in Massachusetts, automobile deaths involving this group soared one hundred and sixty-five percent?
4. Even when there is no drinking involved, you need only study insurance premiums to realize that they consider the young (at least in Massachusetts) the major risk. Here describe vividly a few recent accidents from the newspapers. Emphasize you are not implying drink or reckless driving, but merely lamenting that death should come so tragically to the young, and wondering why. Unfortunately, in any big city, a week's newspapers will usually provide the sickening details. Or, use news items from another town: (a) A week ago . . . (no names or places — just circumstances). (b) Four days ago. . . . (c) The day before yesterday. . . .
5. In the conclusion, underline the moral guilt of reckless driving, of driving after drinking, of speeding in the wee hours on an apparently empty road. The need of teen-age supervision. The need of a commonsense curfew in a home.

Here is a second sample of this "provocative opening" gambit:

They say that if you call out, "Hello, Beautiful!" almost any girl within earshot will turn around. But suppose someone shouted, "Stop, Thief!" — would you halt in your tracks?

Granted, "Stop, Thief!" sounds heavy and flamboyant; still, in the quiet of your conscience it might pull out a few "Stops!" like these:

Stop padding those expense accounts.

Stop kiting insurance claims.

Stop packing hotel towels into your traveling bag.

Stop cheating on those income tax forms.

Stop copying during exams or using bought term papers.

Stop loafing on the job when you should give a decent day's work.

Stop taking things home from the office or the shop: anything from a roll of stamps to a wrench. . . . Can *your* conscience justly call out, "Stop, Thief!"

Each of these can be made more vivid with picturesque details and the conclusion could plead for honesty as the only policy. Most stealing is done without a gun.

IV — True and False

This is another rather obvious device that we have all employed, whether we adverted to the label or not. It goes like this:

First, you debunk a false principle, or perhaps expose the error of a false "fact."

Secondly, you reverse the false page and lay out the truth in bright contrast.

Thirdly, you spotlight the advantages of pursuing the truth.

Suppose, for example, your topic is "Occasion of Sin."

THE FALSE ASSUMPTION

Some people con themselves into thinking that because they are sincere, mature Christians, they can read any books they like, attend any shows they choose, go to any parties they care to, and not be affected at all. (This is one hundred percent false, because bad books and dirty drama do breed bad thoughts, and bad example can induce bad conduct. If you trudge through the mire, some of the mud will stick to your shoes — and wishing it wouldn't will not keep it off.)

THE TRUTH

Original sin is at the bottom of it all. By it our soul was wounded and weakened, so that the soul is now like a run-down constitution, susceptible to any moral illness. Only instead of germs, bacteria, or virus, we have to fear the world, the flesh and the devil.

Any honest man will admit that despite himself he is attracted toward the sensual. He knows from experience that he is vulnerable. He can make excuses for toying with the temptation, but deep down he knows he is playing with dynamite. Since the Fall the inclination to evil is a built-in fire hazard to the soul, and if you leave a window open, the devil will toss in a torch.

CONCLUSION

Admit the grim reality. Keep your guard up and temptation at arm's length. Then you will never have to regret the folly of having been a "daredevil" in the literal sense of that word, or feel the slow agony of bitter remorse. You have not tried to tweak the devil's nose, and so your head can rest on the pillow in peace.

V — Eyewitness

In the ice age of radio, there was a popular program whose chief character had a devastating way of destroying all doubts about the veracity of his colorful story: "I was there, Charlie," he said simply, and skepticism scurried for cover. There is a kindred technique in sermon composition. Instead of simply narrating the incident, you let the details pour out of the persuasive throat of someone who was there on the spot.

Suppose the topic is "The Miracles of Christ." First, you present your introduction and so set the stage. Then one by one the characters march on, something like this:

"My name is Bartimaeus. I used to squat by the town gate, staring with blind eyes, blind since I was born, and rattling my pleading beggar's cup. One day I heard many feet shuffling past. I asked what was happening. They told me Jesus of Nazareth was going by. . . ."

"Never mind *my* name. I am the man who spent thirty-six years crouched at the side of the pool called Bethesda. But I was always too late. By the time I dragged myself to the pool, the water had been stirred, and someone else had got in before me. Then one day this Man from Nazareth they call Jesus. . . ."

"You see this arm? For years and years it was crippled, withered. I could never straighten it out. Then Christ came and touched it, and suddenly it was soft and pliant like my good arm. I do not know how. I just know He touched it. . . ."

"There were ten of us — all lepers. We dared not come near Him. We stood on the other side of the road and called out. He told us to show ourselves to the priest. We set out, doubtfully. But on the way we were cured! The others ran to their villages. I came back to say thanks. . . ."

"My name is Lazarus. . . ."

If you have a fair imagination you can wave your magic wand, and summon up all kinds of situations where make-believe characters can deliver very real and solid truths. Suppose, for instance, a cozy little group are spinning their own Canterbury Tales in hell. Each is telling how he got there.

Gregory: "I lived in the second century, a schoolman. I was a Christian, but then came the Gnostics. They riddled the Gospels with ridicule. They were brains, I tell you. I knew Christianity could not last ten more years. So, I gave up. . . ."

Antoninus: "You think Gnosticism was strong? You should have been there for Arianism, two centuries later. The world woke up one day and found itself Arian. Christianity was doomed and Arianism would replace it. So I got on the bandwagon. . . ."

Placidus: "You two died before Attila and his barbarians. They turned our area of Christianity into one big, charred ruin.

Any church became a bonfire. The Gospel was going up in smoke. At least that's the way it looked when I got out. . . ."

David speaks up: "You talk about the Dark Ages? They called the time when I lived, the Age of Light, the Renaissance. Rome with its worldly cardinals and their pagan art and sometimes dissolute lives — was this the Church of Jesus Christ? This was cancer inside the Mystic Body. I walked out. . . ."

Edward remarks: "I lived right after you, during the Reformation. I saw a half dozen nations drop away from the Church overnight. I saw what was coming. The Rock of Peter would soon be only pebbles. The Church, for all its good intentions, would be nothing more than a footnote in the history books. I got the message and I bailed out. . . ."

And so on, if you wish, through the crises of evolution and biblical criticism. But even as men in each century lost heart and jumped ship, the Bark of Peter plowed through each new rising wave and pushed on with each new crisis bobbing in the distant wake.

VI — Emphasize <u>One</u> Important Word

One advantage of this particular sermon plan is that it helps the preacher memorize his material more easily, and also helps the congregation follow the argument more closely. The preacher does not call attention to the fact that he is underlining one word, but by dint of repetition the audience unconsciously absorbs the emphasis.

You can take a theme as broad as Calvin Coolidge's summary of the sermon he had just heard on sin. Old laconic Cal allowed as how from what he heard, the minister was "agin" it. *Against?*

Sin is wrong because: (1) It is *against* important things. (2) It is *against* important persons.

1. *Against* Important Things:
   a. *Against* the law of God. (Commandments of God, commandments of the Church, conscience — the law written on the human heart.)
   b. *Against* the example of Christ. (His life was an immaculate page. "Which of you shall convict me of sin?" . . . "He went about doing good.")
   c. *Against* the good of our neighbor. (Every sin, from robbery to rape to perjury to murder, hurts our fellowman. And even if it seems to hurt only us, in reality it also hurts the community of which we are members.)
2. *Against* Important Persons:
   a. It is rebellion against the Creator who made us.
   b. It is ingratitude against the Redeemer who died for us.
   c. It is injustice to our neighbor, who is our brother or sister in the family of man.

No man is an island. He is part of the human continent, or a peninsula: literally, almost an island, but not quite. Anything I do, good or evil, has repercussions on those among whom I live.

Or suppose your topic is "The Abuse of Drink." First, of course, you point out that since our Lord used wine for His first miracle and at His Last Supper, the moderate use of alcohol is not wrong. What is forbidden is not the use, but the abuse.

Going back to Cana, the poet Crashaw catches the miracle in a technicolor slide: "The modest water saw its God, and blushed." Here we take some poetic liberty and presume that this blush meant red wine, and we play on the word "red."

Red for all the future abuses of drink!

Red for the red noses of drunks whose purple-veined noses burn before them like altar lamps, because it was of such that St. Paul said, "Their god is their belly."

Red for the red ink of debts piled up in the drunkard's home.

Red for the red traffic lights through which these drunken drivers heedlessly speed.

Red for the red taillights when they park in lonely lanes. When they drive they are a menace to life and limb. When they park they are a menace to morality.

Red for the red blushes of the young girl who discovers that it is not "wine, woman and song," but wine, woman and wrong!

Conclusion: If you are abusing drink, cut it down or cut it out! Lift your eyes to the *red* wounds of Christ. When He groaned, "I thirst," He was doing penance for the abuse of drink. And He was thirsting for your love.

VII — Opposites or Contrasts

Maybe listing these sermon plans tends to lull the reader to drooping eyelids; the prime purpose of such pages, however, is not to entertain but to assist. They are diffidently offered as models so the preacher can glance at them and then take off on his own. They may possibly offer a clue that he has hitherto overlooked. If, as we suspect, he faces the same congregation Sunday after Sunday, he needs new approaches to arouse interest.

It reminds one of that memorable athletic meet where the strongest javelin-thrower was also cross-eyed. It is true he did not win any medals that day, but he certainly kept the crowd alert. In a more conservative sense, that is our purpose, too. So here is another deferential suggestion. Why not sometimes let your talk swing like a suspension bridge between the towers of two opposites or two contrasts? For example, if the theme centered on Pentecost, those contrasts could be two different fires:

1. The opening portrays Pilate's courtyard where Peter huddles close to the fire. Three times he swears he does not even know Christ, though the servant girl taunts him with the accusation that his Galilean accent (probably as dis-

212

tinctive as my Brooklynese) gives him away. This cross-examination can be developed, step by step, so that Peter emerges a skulking coward. At the end, when Christ walks down the stone steps under guard, and gazes at Peter, the latter turns *fiery red* with shame and bursts out of the gate weeping. Coward by the fire!

2. Another "fire," almost two months later. The Upper Room of Jerusalem, the first novena, the Apostles in prayer. The sudden wind and the tongues of fire, a flaming tongue hovering over each Apostle's head, like the scarlet skullcap of the bishops they were to be. Suddenly they find themselves different men. Peter, especially — no longer the coward, but *inflamed* with new courage. He flings open the door, strides out on the balcony, dares to tell the crowd they have crucified Christ, the Son of God. Hero by the fire!

Or another contrast could be developed:

1. The Tower of Babel, where men of the same nation found themselves speaking in different tongues and could not understand one another.

2. The Balcony of Pentecost, where Peter spoke one tongue, his own guttural Aramaic, and men of many nations understood him as if he were speaking their own language.

Or, here is the contrast method applied to another theme:

1. *What Children Swallow.* In Boston's Children's Medical Center, they have an incredible collection of swallowed items, skillfully retrieved, all the way from fraternity pins to safety pins, from thumbtacks to campaign buttons, from pennies to paper clips.

2. *What Adults Swallow.* The slogans and the advertising jingles, the outdoor billboards and the television commercials, the slanted news and the loaded editorials, the subtle suggestions of the new morality: "After all, it is only

natural." (To animals, that is!) "To the pure, all things are pure." (Even impurity?)

Or consider *two failures,* like Judas and Peter:

1. Peter sinned gravely, like Judas. Peter's sin was that he denied Jesus three times, even with an oath. But he repented. He was humble enough to trudge back to Christ. He had fallen deeply; but he got up, came back, asked forgiveness and was reconciled.

2. Judas sinned, too, and (what we sometimes forget) Judas also repented. He confessed he had sinned in betraying innocent blood, and he made restitution by restoring his ill-gotten gains; but he was not humble enough to return to Christ and ask forgiveness from Him. For Judas the sad end was the twisting rope. Peter became the Rock, the very foundation of the new Church.

That allusion to "rock" somehow trapezes over to the Rock of Ages, and suggests that a little talk on the existence of God could neatly fit between the two covers of the Rock of Ages and the Age of Rocks. This contrast is really only a catchy way of saying Creator and Creation.

The first part might point out that rocks are the very floor of our world, the lowest stratum of existence. In fact, that is all they have, existence. Then climb up the old biological ladder to plants which have life, to animals which have motion, to mankind which has intellect. But that rock at the bottom, no matter what its age, no matter how old, had to have a beginning. If once there had been no rock, if once there ever had been nothing at all, then now there would still be only nothing, for out of nothing comes nothing. Therefore, if there is anything here now, there always had to be something. No . . . more than something. There had to be Someone, because in our world, there are more than things, there are intelligent beings. So from the beginning there had to be an Intelligence.

The second part could develop that point. Where there is an

arrangement, there has to be an Arranger. You do not whirl around a bucket of print and find spilled out on the ground before you the first folio version of the first scene in Hamlet. A play leads back to a playwright. And the great globe of the earth with its rhythmic tides and regular seasons, its rotation of day and night, its orderly procession of whirling stars and predictable eclipses, its migration of birds and even the marvel of all that is contained in one tiny bird's egg — to believe that all this is the random result of mere chance is to strain out the gnat of religion and swallow the camel of coincidence.

Shakespeare says there are sermons in stones, and the thoughtful man can read even in the very rocks the slow diary of the Deity.

Or (still thinking in terms of contrasts), a sermon on the very basics of Christianity, sin and salvation, could be hung like a banner between "two trees." One tree, the tree of good and evil in the Garden of Eden, representing temptation and eventual sin. The second tree, the gaunt, bare tree of the cross, the symbol of atonement for sin, the Redemption.

Or let us consider two Communions.

The first, when in the white innocence of childhood a little boy lifts a cherub's face to receive his God, and walks back to his pew, a human ciborium more worthy to contain Him than the precious chalice of Rheims or the Holy Grail.

The last: But sparkling white snow can become slimy gray slush, and when the same boy lifts an aged head to receive Jesus for the last time, he wishes he had lived a nobler life. . . . At least from now on, let us try to live worthy of Him whom we receive!

Sometimes *two characters of history* can be compared or contrasted with dramatic effect:

1. John the Baptist dared to tell Herod it was not right for him to take to wife Herodias (who was already married to Herod's brother, Philip). Similarly, St. John Fisher dared to tell Henry VIII it was not right for him to take Anne

Boleyn (because his own wife, Katharine of Aragón, was still very much alive).

2. Herod's answer was the executioner's ax, and the head of John the Baptist was brought in to the banquet hall on a golden tray. Henry's reaction was the same, and the head of John Fisher dropped into the sanded basket at the Tower of London. (Curiously, when the king's men went to John Fisher's poor rectory, they found before the kneeling bench where he said his daily prayers a cheap plaster-of-parish image of the head of John the Baptist on a gilt plate. He always feared that the day might come when he would have to face the same test, so he prayed for the same courage. After fifteen centuries, the wheel had come full turn.)

VIII — Syllogism

Some words, like "creamy" or "velvet" or "lagoon," seem by their nature pleasant. Syllogism is the other kind, a word that even sounds ugly and formidable, and implies intricacy. But ever since it was housebroken or at least domesticated by that profound thinker, Aristotle, it has carried the weight of the world's arguments.

Philosophers have complicated it with various kinds of figures and modes. But to the preacher it should be as simple as a triangle, with a major, a minor and a conclusion.

However, the difference between a syllogism and a sermon is the difference between the bleak blueprint of a building and the colored postcard view of the completed structure. Or perhaps it would be better to say that the syllogism is the steel skeleton; the sermon the stone and glass skyscraper. What all this means is that in a syllogism plan (if you use this approach), the syllogism should be there, but not too conspicuous. By the audience it should be unconsciously absorbed rather than explicitly noticed.

Try it on so simple a subject as *prayer*:

Major: A good father heeds the pleas of his children.

Minor: God is a good Father.

Conclusion: God will heed our pleas.

MAJOR

Prove this by citing incidents from family life. Whether his little son needs a snowsuit or begs to be taken to the circus, the good father is eager to bring happiness to his child.

MINOR

We do not have to look far to know that God is a good Father. We have only to look about us and see the physical gifts of creation, and look within us to remember the spiritual gifts of Redemption (Jesus our Savior, the Holy Spirit our Sanctifier, the Church our Mother) to realize the goodness of our Father in the material and spiritual world.

CONCLUSION

Such a Father is eager to hear our prayers, if they be, in His unerring judgment, for our final good. If He does not grant our pleas, it is not that He is not good, but that in the circumstances our requests are bad, or at least not the best in the overall view of eternity.

Note: If this conclusion seems to hedge, it should be made clear that in any sermon the preacher should take into consideration the obvious difficulties that may go scurrying through the hearer's mind. Sometimes the preacher should come forth with an outright rebuttal, sometimes with more detailed explanation, and sometimes with the open admission that we poor human beings — priest or pope — just do not know.

If we knew as much as God, would we not also be God? Often we simply have to take His word; and if we cannot take His, whose word can we take?

217

One thinks with something between a headshake and a smile of that passenger on the storm-tossed liner who nervously approached the captain. "Tell me, sir," he said, "just what is our true situation?" The captain paused and said, "If you really want to know the truth, we are in the hands of God." The passenger turned pale. "Is it as bad as that?"

But back to syllogisms. Personally I was never much of a syllogism man, mainly because it always seemed to me that in the ordinary sermon the underlying syllogism is already accepted by the people. They believe the truths proposed, but sometimes the truths need fuller explanation and sometimes the people need stronger motivation.

"Premises, premises" can be as barren as "promises, promises." The important aim is to keep to the topic and not wander. But you can do this without making the homily an arid exercise in logic. As long as you keep to the theme, you can approach it from many directions, just as the main avenues of the city of Washington are supposed to lead into the Capitol like the spokes of a great wheel. For example, I would be at a loss how to fit neatly within the framework of a syllogism the points I might like to bring out in a sermon on "Why We Catholics Believe in the Real Presence." My plan could emerge something like this:

1. Consider *what* Christ said: "This is my body." Not "like my body" or "a symbol of my body" or "a souvenir of my body." But, "my body."
2. Consider *when* He said it: At the most solemn time of His life. The night before He died. At the edge of death men are grimly serious. Then a man speaks straight and true.
3. Consider *how* He prepared His disciples for hearing it. At least a year before this, He had promised He would give them His flesh to eat. He did not spring it on them suddenly. And at that time, when they heard Him speak of giving His flesh to eat, some openly said they could not take it, and they walked with Him no more. Did He on that oc-

casion call them back and assure them He did not mean it literally, or that they had misunderstood? He did not. He had spoken clearly; they had understood rightly. He had to let them go.

4. Consider *His right* to say it: He was God. His miracles had all marched before, proving His power. This Last Supper and Real Presence came only the night before He died, proving His love. But the Apostles knew that He who had changed water into wine could by that same power change wine into His own blood. They knew that He who had taken the pale, waxen hand of the dead daughter of Jairus and lifted her up to life, could with that same power breathe life into the pale bread. They knew that He who had concealed His dazzling divinity everywhere except on Mount Tabor, when suddenly He shone like the very sun, could *have* His divinity and still *hide* it in the Sacred Host. . . .

Many sermons, if you take the trouble to break them down, are really syllogisms, even though the title might throw you off. Actually the reasoning or the argument glides beneath the surface, all the more skillful because it is not evident, the title being only the conning tower.

Some men find the syllogism form cramping. No problem: just select *any* method or plan that puts you at ease. In the homiletic pool, there are all sort of strokes, from dog paddle to butterfly. The main thing is to go forward and not merely tread water. One theme, one beginning, one middle, one end — this is the simple structure of the finest sermon ever preached.

IX — The Evil: Its Cause and Cure

A commercially minded evangelist once remarked that a good sermon is one that makes the audience laugh a little, cry a little and, at the end, feel a warm glow inside. Any sincere preacher would scornfully retort that on the menu of pulpit oratory, such a dish would be only snow pudding: empty, frothy and practically nothing. Wit and pathos and a touch of sentiment are valid ingredients; but they are not meat and potatoes, not the staple foods. The ideal purpose of the sermon is always to produce action, either by doing something we have neglected to do, or by ceasing to do something that we never should have done.

Let's suppose that our topic is "Anger." The sermon's goal is to have the congregation practice self-control:

1. *Portray the evil* (losing one's temper). If only we could show the angry man some home movies of his outburst: the bulging eyes, the flaming cheeks, the teeth gleaming like tusks — he would see himself not so much as a human being but as an infuriated animal. If he could hear a sound track of his explosion, the screamed profanity, the incoherent insults — like a little tin god roaring his thunder and hurling his lightning from his own private heaven. St. Thomas Aquinas claims that the first reaction of an angry man is pleasure, the animal joy of pounding a table, the sweeping relief of sulfuric outbursts, the thrill of going native. Hence anger's appeal.

2. *Cause of anger* (anything that opposes our own sweet will). A childish, undisciplined, trigger-happy temper, with no safety catch whatever. An impetuous, immediate, almost automatic response to an unpleasant situation, instead of trying to see both sides.

3. *Results of anger* (like a sudden tornado, one abrupt outburst of anger can flatten trees of friendship that have stood for fifty years). You cannot call back a bullet from a gun nor a word from an angry mouth. Wounds can be bandaged, but anger leaves scars that can never be painted over.

4. *Cure for anger* (easy to say, hard to do: self-restraint). Holding back the wild horses of passion. Walking away

from the scene, even in so prosaic a way as going into the kitchen for a drink of water. In the business world, lose your temper and you may lose a customer or even your job. At home you may do worse: you may break a dear one's heart. The competent pilot rides above the storm.

X — Allegory or Parable

This is a tricky one. The French rhetoricians have a saying, "In crystal palace / Allegory dwells," meaning, I suppose, that if you are going to give us an allegory, make certain it is crystal-clear.

An obscure allegory is like a rain-blurred windshield: you cannot see where you are headed. A homily ought not to be a guessing game.

Technically, an allegory is an extended or prolonged comparison. The difficulty is that, like pulled taffy, the longer you draw it out, the thinner (and sometimes the stickier) it becomes. Often these allegorical sermons are more to be admired for their art than imitated for their practicality. They resemble one of those tiny carved ivory ships you see in a museum, with sails and flags and every delicate detail; but if you drop it in the water, it sinks.

In homiletics an allegory carried too far is a contrived, artificial device that may occasionally raise an eyebrow, but rarely move a heart or sway a will.

Still, within limits, it has possibilities to spur interest. We have just mentioned little ships. Try this bigger one:

INTRODUCTION

Ever since Christ, pressed by the crowd, stepped into Peter's boat and preached from its prow, as from a pulpit, spiritual men have looked upon a church as a ship.

DEVELOPMENT

Like a ship, a church always has a name. Like a ship, a church usually has a bell. Like a ship, a church often has a tall spire soaring up like a mast and topped with the tiny yardarm of a cross.

Show me a Catholic church, and I shall show you:

1. A fishing ship where, in the finely meshed nets of the confessional screens, sinners are caught for the glory of God.
2. A cargo ship where prayers and hymns and earnest resolutions and Masses and Communions and rich indulgences are stored away in the hold for shipment to eternity.
3. A battleship where from the pulpit thunder the guns of God, blasting vice and defending virtue.
4. A passenger ship where the faithful are carried over the dark, jagged rocks and storm-tossed waters of this pagan world to the safe harbor of heaven.

DIFFERENCE

But a Catholic church is unlike other conventional ships in one particularly striking way: The average passenger ship separates the passengers into first class, cabin class, tourist. Once there was, alas, the infamous steerage (by which many of our parents came to America). But in the ship of the parish church there is neither steerage nor peerage, because:

1. *A church is a modern Bethlehem.* Just as of yore kings and shepherds, Wise Men and peasants, knelt shoulder to shoulder in the straw of the stable, so today the wealthy and the poor, the learned and the unlettered, kneel side by side in the parish pews.
2. *A church is a modern Calvary.* Just as at Calvary there stood beneath the cross the stainless Mary of Nazareth and the stained Mary of Magdala, so within the walls of a church you will find both saints and sinners, the innocent and the repentant.
3. *A church is a modern Nazareth.* At any time we can

slip in out of the cold modern world (so often it is only the old paganism with shining new plumbing) and warm ourselves before the fire of Faith, and quietly greet the Holy Family that lives there: Jesus, really there in the Blessed Sacrament, and Mary and Joseph at least in shrine or statue.

CONCLUSION

Each individual church is just one of the fleet of churches behind the flagship, the Bark of Peter. That ship, the Bark of Peter, the Universal Church, will always sail on, plowing through each new storm and leaving each new heresy behind like a chip in its foaming wake. The Ship of Peter will survive, not because the clergy are particularly clever, or the laity especially pious, or because of financial wealth or diplomatic skill or military might, but for one sole reason: our Lord, Jesus Christ, is aboard! This ship cannot sink. He has promised that He will be with her till the end of time.

Another sermon treatment, best reserved for rare occasions lest it sound too "hammy," is the use of the vivid or *historical present*. Thus a talk on the rosary might begin:

"It is the seventh of October 1573. Into the Gulf of Lepanto sweeps a huge Turkish fleet, every sail bright with a crimson crescent. Round the far point the Christian fleet approaches, hastily gathered together, pitifully small. In the prow of the flagship stands Don Juan of Austria. . . ."

This picture-to-yourself approach can produce a simple, bright, action-packed talk; but in using it one walks the tightrope between the childish and the over-dramatic. Cynics contend it is the ideal vehicle for a homily in a foreign language, because it stays far away from all subjunctives and pluperfects. Many good preachers adopt it almost automatically when describing some colorful scene and then quietly return to the main theme.

Finally (honest!), there is what you might call the "Tenement Talk" which consists of a basement, a roof and four or five stories. The basement is the introduction, the stories are stories in the other sense (anecdotes allegedly relevant), and the roof is the conclusion, often flat. As we grow older and encounter more experiences, we all tend to fall into our anecdotage. A severe drawback to this method is that a string of stories is apt to shortchange the congregation on information and argument. There is neither clear explanation nor persuasive motivation.

No one is likely to deny that a sermon woven of reasonably good stories is easy to learn, easy to deliver and easy to listen to. But isn't such a sermon often like a tray of cream puffs — attractive and appealing, but with no spiritual protein? In homiletics, sometimes the easiest method is miles removed from the best.

At least that is the gut conviction in this corner. Should your view be the exact opposite, I shall not challenge it. Nowhere in this book have I wanted to take the position of a sharpshooter kneeling on a neighboring rooftop and sniping at a rectory window. All I wanted to do was to offer (not thrust down your throat) some mild suggestions drained from almost fifty years of preaching. Experience is just a velvet word for lessons learned from mistakes, and in reminiscing about mine I only hoped to pass on a little homily help. I never promised you a prose garden.

Just one final thing. How about a little prayer for this well-meaning padre who wishes he could begin all over again? He has to be close to the ultimate threshold and needs all the backing he can get. Thanks!

INDEX

Dostoyevsky, Feodor Mikhailovich — 98
Duncan, Isadora — 22

Einstein, Albert — 190
Elijah — 149
Emerson, Ralph Waldo — 65, 118

Father Damien — 65
Ferber, Edna — 120
Fisher, St. John — *See* John Fisher
Fosdick, Harry Emerson — 15f, 32
Francis of Assisi, St. — 196

Gabriel — 199
Gibbons, James — 34
Grant, Cary — 190
Guest, Edgar — 73
Gutenberg, Johann — 81

Häring, Bernard — 80
Harrison, Rex — 21
Henry VIII — 215
Herod — 215f
Holmes, Oliver Wendell — 153
Homer — 132
Houdini, Harry — 50

Irving, Sir Henry — 178
Iscariot — *See* Judas Iscariot

Jairus — 148, 219
James (the Apostle), St. — 148f
Jesus Christ — 16f, 25, 31, 43, 47ff, 58, 70, 93, 103ff, 113ff, 119, 132ff, 141, 148f, 151, 155, 159, 164, 171, 181f, 193, 204, 209ff, 221f
John (the Apostle), St. — 148f
John the Baptist, St. — 215f
John Fisher, St. — 215f
John XXIII — 202
Joseph, St. — 98, 107, 183, 223
Judas Iscariot — 98, 105, 159, 214
Juvenal — 201

Katharine of Aragón — 215
Keats, John — 97
Kelly, Grace — 61
Kilmer, Joyce — 155
King David — *See* David
King Henry VIII — *See* Henry VIII
King Louis the Great — *See* Louis I
Kipling, Rudyard — 114
Küng, Hans — 80, 138

Lacordaire, Jean Baptiste Henri — 90, 197
Lazarus — 95, 98, 209
Lewis, Sinclair — 25

Newman, John Henry — 101, 182
Newton, Joseph — 87

O'Connell, Daniel — 72
O. Henry [pseudonym of William Sydney Porter] — 101, 155
Oliver Plunket, St. — 153
Olivier, Laurence — 102
Our Lady — *See* Mary
Our Lord — *See* Jesus Christ
Our Redeemer — *See* Jesus Christ
Our Savior — *See* Jesus Christ

Padre Antonio — *See* Anthony of Padua
Patrick, St. — 153, 155, 183
Paul, St. — 16, 35, 211
Paul VI — 202
Pepys, Samuel — 84
Peter, St. — 96, 135, 148f, 182, 210ff, 221ff
Philip, St. — 134
Philip Herod — 215
Phillips, Wendell — 28, 48
Pike, James Albert — 32f
Pilate — *See* Pontius Pilate
Pius X — 155
Plunket, St. Oliver — *See* Oliver Plunket
Ponce de León, Juan — 50
Pontius Pilate — 212
Porter, William Sydney — *See* O. Henry
Princess Grace (of Monaco) — *See* Kelly, Grace

Queen Victoria — *See* Victoria
Quintilian — 44, 126, 139, 160

Rahner, Karl — 80, 138
Raphael Santi (or Sanzio) — 122
Richelieu, Armand Jean du Plessio, duc de — *See* Cardinal Richelieu
Romulo, Carlos — 178
Roosevelt, Franklin Delano — 109
Ruskin, John — 197
Russell, Rosalind — 21

Santi — *See* Raphael Santi
Sanzio — *See* Raphael Santi
Saul — 105, 171
Savonarola, Girolamo — 88
Schillebeeckx, Edward — 80
Scott, Sir Walter — 52, 101
Shakespeare, William — 9, 52, 100, 107, 115f, 118, 154, 215
Shaw, George Bernard — 22, 175
Sheed, Frank (Francis J.) — 14, 135, 160
Sheen, Fulton J. — 33f, 46, 76f, 161, 171, 198
Stevenson, Robert Louis — 101

Talleyrand, Charles Maurice de — 65
Teilhard de Chardin, Pierre — 80
Thackeray, William Makepeace — 50, 78, 101
Thomas Aquinas, St. — 139, 220
Thompson, Francis — 114
Thoreau, Henry David — 119

Tillich, Paul — 138
Twain, Mark — *See* Mark Twain

Victoria — 13

Walker, Jimmy (James John) — 109
Wesley, Charles — 19, 177

Xenophon — 132

Zacchaeus — 82